Easy FrontPage™ 97

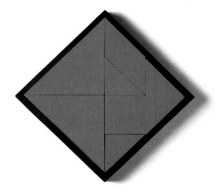

by Dennis Jones

Easy FrontPage 97

Library of Congress Catalog Card Number: 97-65023

International Standard Book Number: 0-7897-1224-5

99 98 97   8 7 6 5 4 3 2 1

Interpretation of the printing code: the rightmost double-digit number is the year of the book's first printing; the rightmost single-digit number is the number of the book's printing. For example, a printing code of 97-1 shows that this copy of the book was printed during the first printing of the book in 1997.

Screen reproductions in this book were created by means of the program Collage Complete from Inner Media, Inc, Hollis, NH.

Printed in the United States of America.

Dedication

To Sandi

Credits

President
Roland Elgey

Publisher
Joseph B. Wikert

Editorial Services Director
Elizabeth Keaffaber

Managing Editor
Sandy Doell

Director of Marketing
Lynn E. Zingraf

Acquisitions Editor
Jane K. Brownlow

Technical Specialist
Nadeem Muhammed

Product Development Specialist
Benjamin Milstead

Technical Editor
Kyle Bryant

Production Editor
Jim Bowie

Book Designers
Barbara Kordesh
Ruth Harvey

Cover Designer
Dan Armstrong

Production Team
Brian Grossman
Bob LaRoche
Julie Searls
Staci Somers
Lisa Stumpf

Indexer
Chris Barrick

Composed in *Syntax* and *New Century Schoolbook* by Que Corporation

We'd Like to Hear from You!

As part of our continuing effort to produce books of the highest possible quality, Que would like to hear your comments. To stay competitive, we *really* want you, as a computer book reader and user, to let us know what you like or dislike most about this book or other Que products.

You can mail comments, ideas, or suggestions for improving future editions to the address below, or send us a fax at (317) 581-4663. Our staff and authors are available for questions and comments through our Internet site, at **http://www.quecorp.com**, and Macmillan Computer Publishing also has a forum on CompuServe (type **GO QUEBOOKS** at any prompt).

In addition to exploring our forum, please feel free to contact me personally to discuss your opinions of this book: I'm **bmilstead@que.mcp.com** on the Internet, and **102121,1324** on CompuServe.

Thanks in advance—your comments will help us to continue publishing the best books available on new computer technologies in today's market.

Benjamin Milstead
Product Director
Que Corporation
201 W. 103rd Street
Indianapolis, Indiana 46290
USA

About the Author

Dennis Jones is a freelance technical writer, software trainer, and novelist, and is coauthor of Que's *Special Edition Using Microsoft FrontPage 97*. He also teaches creative writing at the University of Waterloo, Canada, and lives in Waterloo.

Acknowledgments

I'd like to thank Jane Brownlow and Ben Milstead of the Que editorial staff for helping me get this book done to a pretty tight schedule. And, I'd like to acknowledge the long-term support of Neil Randall, who encouraged me to get into this business in the first place.

Trademarks

All terms mentioned in this book that are known to be trademarks or service marks have been appropriately capitalized. Que Corporation cannot attest to the accuracy of this information. Use of a term in this book should not be regarded as affecting the validity of any trademark or service mark.

Contents

Contents

Part VI: Maintaining Your Web   186

Index   204

Introduction

What You Can Do with Microsoft FrontPage 97

Microsoft FrontPage 97 is an integrated World Wide Web site-creation package. Its main parts are a program called FrontPage Explorer, which is for Web creation and Web-site management, and another called FrontPage Editor, which you use to create Web pages. Also included with FrontPage 97 is the FrontPage Bonus Pack, which includes a Web server called the Microsoft Personal Web Server; a graphics package called Image Composer; and the Microsoft Internet Explorer Web browser. With FrontPage 97, you can create a complete Web site on your PC, and link that site to the World Wide Web and the Internet.

Here are some of the specific tasks you can accomplish with FrontPage 97:

- Create Webs into which you can place your own Web pages. You can create these Webs empty, or use the supplied templates and Web wizards to set up Webs for purposes like customer service, discussions, and project development.

- Create pages for your Web. These can be blank pages, into which you put your own material. Or you can use the supplied templates and Page Wizards to set up preformatted pages that you can then customize.

- Set up the Microsoft Personal Web Server to make your Webs available to other people connected to the World Wide Web and the Internet. To do this, of course, your PC must have a connection to the Internet.

- Use the Personal Web Server to view your Web over the Internet in a browser, just as your visitors will. This is extremely valuable for checking the appearance and behavior of your Web site.

- Check for broken links within your site and to other sites on the World Wide Web. When you find a broken link, FrontPage Explorer makes it easy to fix.

- Use the To Do List to organize and monitor the work of creating and maintaining your Web site.

Most of the work of creating pages for your Web is done with FrontPage Editor. With this powerful program—it works very much like a Windows word processor—you can:

- Lay out text, with full support for fonts, character formatting, character size, and text color.

- Use lists. FrontPage Editor gives you bulleted lists, numbered lists, and definition lists, which you can use to organize the information you want to provide for the visitors to your site.

- Improve your writing with spell checking and a thesaurus. Both of these writing tools closely resemble those built into Microsoft Word.

- Insert hyperlinks into your pages. Hyperlinks connect the pages of your Web to other pages in it, and to Web sites out there on the World Wide Web.

- Use images. FrontPage Editor's tools allow you to easily import images into your Webs, and quickly place them on your pages. You can turn images into hyperlinks, too.

- Make image maps easily. These special graphics are used for hyperlinking, and you can have several links residing in different parts of the image.

- Create your own graphics, and modify existing ones. Microsoft Image Composer, part of the Bonus Pack, lets you assemble new graphics from a large library of supplied images. Or you can take an existing graphic and process it to look like an Impressionist painting, a pastel, a watercolor, and so on.

- Add sound to a page. Putting a sound file into your Web page is as simple as importing the file into your Web and setting up a link to it. FrontPage Editor also lets you add Background Sound, a feature supported by the Microsoft Internet Explorer 3.0 browser.

- Add video to a page. All you need to do is import a video file into your Web, then insert a link to it onto your page. FrontPage Editor also lets you add in-line video for people who use Microsoft Internet Explorer 3.0.

Big Screen

At the beginning of each task is a large screen that shows how the computer screen will look after you complete the procedure that follows in that task. Sometimes the screen shows a feature discussed in that task, however, such as a shortcut menu.

TASK 23

Making a Bulleted or Numbered List

"Why would I do this?"

Lists are excellent for helping you integrate presentation and content in your Web pages. Bulleted lists are for items that require no particular ordering. Numbered lists are used for tables of contents, for establishing a rank order, for a set of instructions, or for any information where relative importance needs to be shown.

24

Step-by-Step Screens

Each task includes a screen shot for each step of a procedure that shows how the computer screen will look at each step in the process.

Task 23: Making a Bulleted or Numbered List

1 To insert an item into an existing list, click immediately to the right of the preceding item, press **Enter**, and type the new item. Then slide the mouse pointer to above or below the list, and click to place the insertion point outside the list.

Puzzled?

To delete an item from a list, drag across it and press the **Delete** key to remove the text. Then press the **Delete** key again. This removes the bullet or number.

Puzzled?

You may find that you are having trouble performing a task. The "Puzzled?" sections tell you how to get out of a challenging situation.

2 To make a numbered list, open the List Properties dialog box as you did in Step 1. In that dialog box, click the tab labeled "Numbered." Then click the page icon that shows the numbering style you want. Then click **OK**, and the number 1 appears on the page.

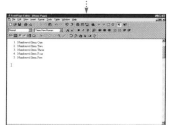

3 Start typing your list, pressing **Enter** at the end of each item. When you've finished, press **Enter** twice to stop inserting numbered items. To insert an item into a numbered list, use the technique in Step 4. Note the numbering is adjusted automatically when you do this. ■

Missing Link

A fast way to turn bullets or numbering on or off is to click the **Bulleted List** and **Numbered List** buttons on the toolbar.

25

Missing Link

Many tasks contain other short notes that tell you a little more about certain procedures. These notes define terms, explain other options, refer you to other sections when applicable, and so on.

PART I

Getting Started with Webs and Web Pages

PART I OF THIS BOOK INTRODUCES YOU to Microsoft FrontPage 97. You learn how to install FrontPage, how to create Webs and Web pages from templates and wizards, and how to use the Microsoft Personal Web Server to view your Webs over the Internet.

Web "sites"—which are organized collections of Web pages, such as you'll learn to produce in this book—exist on computers, ranging from really big ones to the humble desktop PC. But no matter how exotic the computer on which it exists, a Web site is accessible to millions of users because that computer is hooked up to the Internet through telephone lines or special high-speed data lines. (You can get by quite well with just a phone line, so don't worry.)

The Internet itself is a vast network of computers connected by various telecommunications methods. A particular part of the Internet is referred to as the World Wide Web, though many people use the two terms interchangeably. The World Wide Web is an enormous collection of individual Web sites, linked together by a method called "hyperlinking." Within each site are "pages," which can contain images, text, hyperlinks, sound, video, and even computer programs. When you're "surfing the Net" it's these pages that you see in a browser like Netscape Navigator or Microsoft Internet Explorer.

Until recently, creating a Web site hasn't been especially easy. Doing so involved specialized technical knowledge, and an acquaintance with a computer language called the HyperText Markup Language, or "HTML" for short. With FrontPage 97, though, you don't need to know HTML, nor do you need to be a telecommunications guru. Using FrontPage isn't unlike using a word processor, and with it you can build quality Web sites even if you've never used the Internet for anything more than e-mail and Web surfing.

Before you can install FrontPage and use it, you need to be sure you have all the hardware and software it requires. A decent setup would include:

- A PC with Windows 95 or NT installed—FrontPage runs only with these two operating systems. Absolutely the slowest machine you could get away with would be a 486-66, and if you're going to use FrontPage's graphics program (called Image Composer) you're going to do a lot of waiting with a 486. A Pentium 75 with a decent graphics card will let you work without too many long delays.

- 16MB of RAM, minimum. FrontPage will run a lot faster with more RAM than that—go for 32MB if you can.

- A good-size hard drive. FrontPage itself needs about 30-50MB, depending on which parts of it you install, but you'll need lots of room for the Webs you create, and for the files included in them. Think in terms of at least 200MB of free space.

- A CD-ROM drive—FrontPage 97 comes only on CD.

- A sound card, so you can test the audio files you link to your pages.

- A modem, capable of at least 14,400 bps. A 28,800 bps modem would be better.

- A connection to the Internet through the modem or through a network.

- As for browsers, FrontPage comes with Internet Explorer 3.0. (If you already have that on your system, you don't have to install it again.) For professional-style Web development, though, you should be capable of viewing your pages in the major browsers. If you install both Internet Explorer and Netscape Navigator, you'll cover most users.

TASK 1

Installing FrontPage 97

"Why would I do this?"

When you install FrontPage 97 and the FrontPage 97 Bonus pack for the first time, you have some choices. In this task, we'll step through the procedure for getting FrontPage up and running, with the FrontPage "client"—that is, the essential FrontPage program—installed, along with Microsoft Image Composer, the Microsoft Personal Web Server, and Microsoft Internet Explorer 3.0. These four programs will give you all the tools you need to work through the tasks in this book.

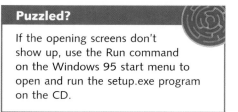

1 Put the FrontPage 97 CD into your CD-ROM drive and close the tray. The CD has Autorun, so you'll see the FrontPage opening screens after a few seconds. In the opening screen, click the large button labeled **FrontPage 97 Installation**.

Puzzled?

If the opening screens don't show up, use the Run command on the Windows 95 start menu to open and run the setup.exe program on the CD.

2 A FrontPage 97 Installation dialog appears, asking if you want to install the Microsoft Personal Web Server. Click **Yes**.

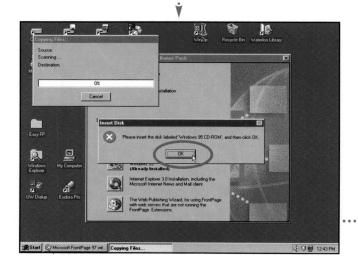

3 You'll see activity on-screen. Then the install program will ask for your Windows 95 CD-ROM. Remove the FrontPage CD from the drive and replace it with the Windows 95 CD. Close the drive tray, wait about 10 seconds until Windows finds the CD, and click **OK**. When the dialog box asks you to restart your PC, do so. FrontPage prompts you to reinsert the FrontPage CD. Do so, and after a few seconds the FrontPage 97 installation dialog box reappears (you don't need to click the OK button in the prompt dialog box).

4 In the installation dialog box, click the **FrontPage 97 Installation** button again. Then follow the instructions on the screen to complete the installation of the FrontPage "client" program. (To work best with this book, you should use the Destination Path suggested by the install program, and use the Typical installation, not the Custom.) When the Setup Complete dialog box appears, click **Finish**.

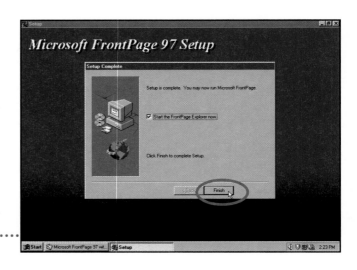

5 FrontPage Explorer starts up, and determines your PC's "hostname" and "address," which it needs so it can set up your Webs. After this has been done, FrontPage Explorer is still open. Since we want to install more software, we'll close FrontPage Explorer. Do this by first clicking the **Cancel** button of the Getting Started with Microsoft FrontPage dialog box. Then open FrontPage Explorer's **File** menu and click the **Exit** option.

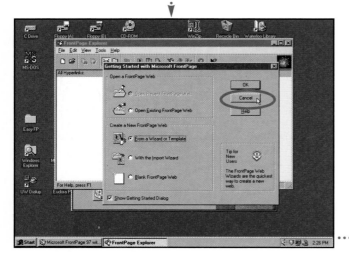

6 The installation dialog box is still open. Click the button labeled **Microsoft Image Composer**. In the Microsoft Image Composer Setup dialog box, click the **Typical Install** button. Then follow the instructions on the screen to install the software. When Image Composer installation is complete, the installation dialog box will reappear. If you already have Microsoft Internet Explorer 3.0 on your PC, installation is complete. Close the installation dialog box, and remove the CD from the drive. Otherwise, continue with Steps 7 and 8.

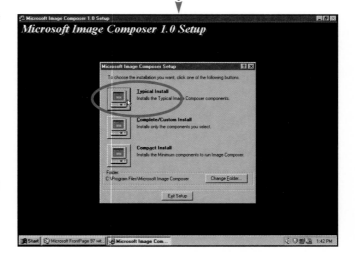

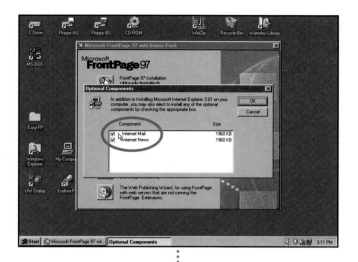

7 In the installation dialog box, click **Internet Explorer 3.0**. To customize the installation, click **Yes** in the Internet Explorer Setup dialog box. Then, in the Optional Components dialog box, click in the Internet Mail and/or Internet News check boxes to check or uncheck them. Click **OK** to complete the installation. When prompted to restart your PC, do so. After restart, close the installation dialog box and remove the FrontPage CD. You now have a new icon on your desktop, labeled "The Internet."

8 If you've never installed Internet Explorer on your system, you'll need to run the Internet Connection Wizard. Double-click the new "The Internet" icon. When the Wizard dialog box opens, click **Next** to go to the Setup Options dialog box. Here you have a choice of Automatic, Manual, and Current options. Click in the appropriate white circle (called a "radio button") to mark it black, then proceed by clicking **Next**. If your PC is already hooked up to the Internet, choosing Current is your best choice. The other options are beyond the scope of this book. ∎

Missing Link

The server installs so that it starts up automatically whenever you start Windows 95. Task 14, "Running the Microsoft Personal Web Server," shows you how to change this behavior.

Puzzled?

The prompt dialog box asking for the FrontPage CD may still be on the screen. Click **Cancel** to get rid of it.

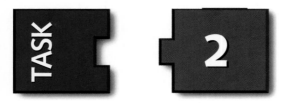

Creating a Basic Web with FrontPage Explorer

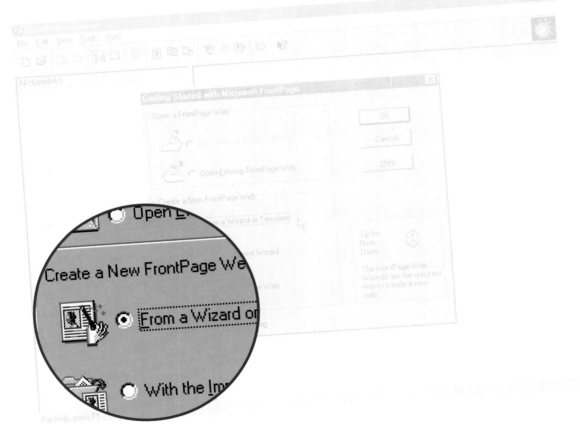

"Why would I do this?"

Before you start creating Web pages with FrontPage 97, you need a place to put them. We call this "place" a FrontPage Web (or "Web," for short) and it's stored on the hard disk of your PC. The individual Web pages are saved in this FrontPage Web and are considered part of it.

With FrontPage 97, setting up a basic Web is very simple. This task tells you how to start FrontPage, and create your Web.

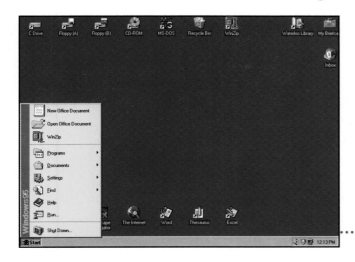

1 Click the Start button to display the Start menu.

2 Slide the mouse onto the Programs menu. Windows displays the Programs menu choices. These choices will be different on each computer, depending on what programs are installed on each machine.

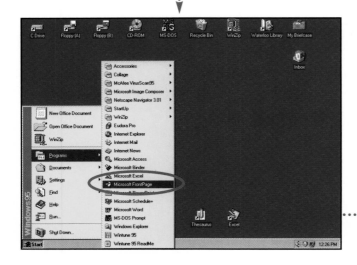

3 Slide the mouse to highlight the Microsoft FrontPage icon. Click **Microsoft FrontPage** once with the left mouse button. FrontPage starts and the Getting Started with Microsoft FrontPage dialog box appears. This dialog box is part of FrontPage Explorer. You use FrontPage Explorer to set up your Web, before you start using FrontPage Editor to create pages.

4 In the Getting Started with Microsoft FrontPage dialog box, look at the white circle (called a radio button) next to "From a Wizard or Template." The radio button should have a black dot in it to show it's selected. If it isn't marked with a black dot, click once inside the radio button to mark it as selected. Click **OK**, and the New FrontPage Web dialog box opens.

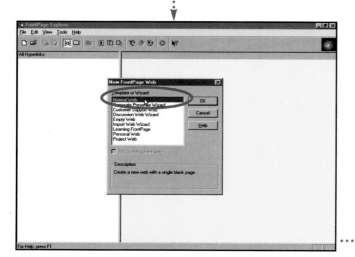

5 The New FrontPage Web dialog box has several basic designs (called "templates") you can use as the start of a Web. We'll set up a Normal Web, so click once on **Normal Web**. Then click **OK** to make the Normal Web Template dialog box appear.

6 To function properly, FrontPage needs the location (or "address") of the Web server that will make your Web accessible to you and the world. FrontPage's setup program finds this out automatically, so you'll see the server name already supplied in the Web Server or File Location text box. FrontPage also needs a name for the Web, so type a suitable name into the Name of New FrontPage Web text box (don't use spaces). Then click **OK** to begin creating the Web.

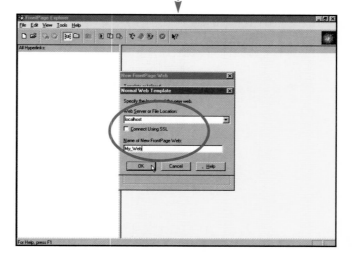

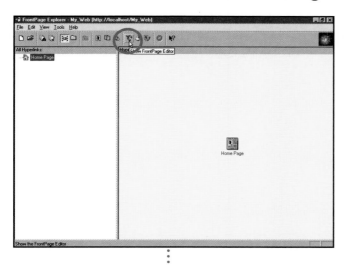

7 Presto! FrontPage Explorer creates the
Web for you, and opens it. You see a window with right and left sections, called
"Views." Your new Home Page has been set
up automatically, and you'll see an icon for
it in each View. But since your new Home
Page has nothing in it yet, you'll want to
add some content. We call this activity
"editing a page." To get started, slide the
mouse pointer along the toolbar to the
Show FrontPage Editor icon. Then click
once to start FrontPage Editor.

8 When the FrontPage Editor window
appears, slide the mouse to the menu bar
and click once on **File**. When the File
menu appears, click once on **Open** to
reveal the Open File dialog box. Then click
once on the file name **Default.htm** to
select it, and finish by clicking **OK**. This
loads your Home Page into FrontPage
Editor's workspace.

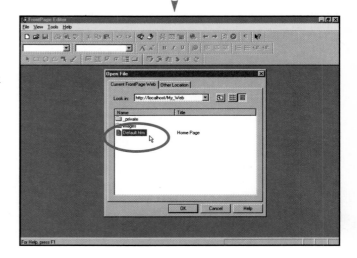

Puzzled?

If you have problems identifying
an icon, leave the mouse pointer
sitting on it for a couple of
seconds.
A ToolTip will appear, giving you the
name of the icon.

Missing Link

All Web pages have two iden-
tifiers: the Page Title, and the
file name of the page. The Page
Title is just a label for the page,
and appears in the title bar of a
browser. In the example we're using,
Default.htm is the file name of the
page, and "Home Page" is its Page
Title.

9 Now you can add to the page or change it (edit it). For now, we'll learn how to save and close a changed page. Just press the spacebar once; doing this changes the page. Now, click **File** on the menu bar. When the menu appears, slide the mouse down to **Save** and click once. To close the page (remove it from the workspace) click **File** on the menu bar, then click **Close**. If you've finished with FrontPage Editor, click **File** on the menu bar, then click **Exit**. This closes the editor and returns you to FrontPage Explorer.

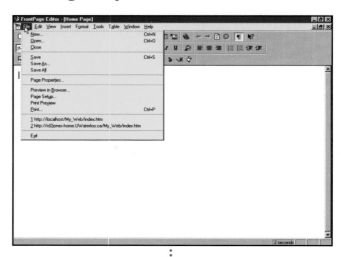

10 When you're finished working on your Web, you close FrontPage Explorer by clicking **File** on the menu bar, then clicking **Exit**. ■

Puzzled?

If you look at the Windows 95 Taskbar after closing FrontPage Explorer, you'll see a tiny globe-and-monitor icon at the right end, near the time display. This shows that the Microsoft Personal Web Server is still running. This is so people can get at your Web, assuming you're connected to the Internet. To shut down the server, refer to Task 14, "Running the Microsoft Personal Web Server."

TASK 3

Creating a Blank Web Page with FrontPage Editor

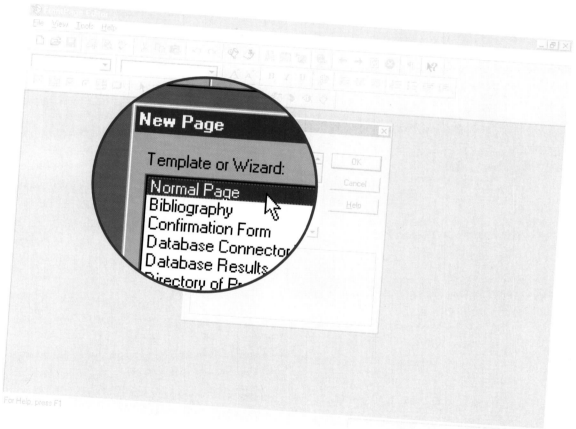

"Why would I do this?"

In Task 2, you learned that creating a Normal Web automatically also created a Home Page. But you'll want more than one page in your Web site, if only because several small Web pages are easier to maintain than a few large

ones. The most basic page is a blank one (which FrontPage Editor calls "Normal") which you can customize completely to your needs and tastes. The usual term for changing the content of a page is "editing."

Task 3: Creating a Blank Web Page with FrontPage Editor

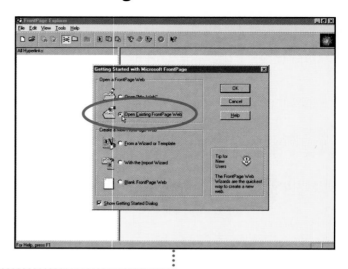

1 We'll assume you're going to add pages to an existing Web. To open the Web, start FrontPage Explorer, as you did in Task 2. Then look at the Getting Started With Microsoft FrontPage dialog box to find the radio button labeled "Open Existing FrontPage Web." Click the radio button, then click **OK**.

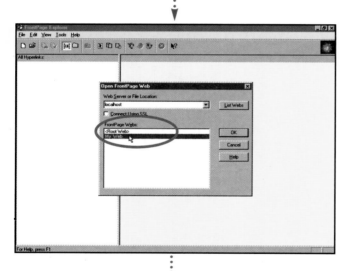

2 The Web Server or File Location text box will have the server address found by FrontPage during installation, so you can ignore it. Click the **List Webs** button to show the Webs available on this server. Then, in the FrontPage Webs list box, click the name of the Web you want to open. Then click **OK**.

> **Puzzled?**
>
> If you don't see the Getting Started with Microsoft FrontPage dialog box, do this to open a Web: click **File** on the menu bar, then click **Open FrontPage Web**.

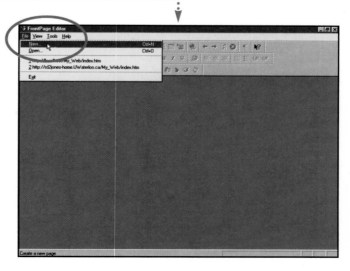

3 When FrontPage Explorer opens the Web, click the Show FrontPage Editor button on the toolbar (you learned this in Task 2, remember?). FrontPage Editor starts, with no page in the workspace. Now slide the mouse to the menu bar and click **File**. When the menu bar appears, click **New**. The New Page dialog box appears.

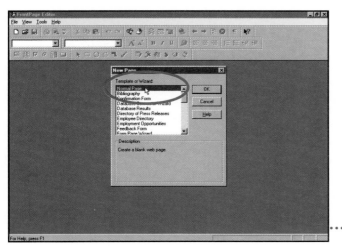

4 Slide the mouse to the list box in the New Page dialog box, then click **Normal Page** to select it. Next, click **OK**.

5 When the new page appears, you can begin editing it. First, you should save it with a suitable Page Title and file name. Click **File** on the menu bar, then click **Save As**. Type suitable names into the Page Title text box and the File Path Within Your FrontPage Web text box. Then click **OK**.

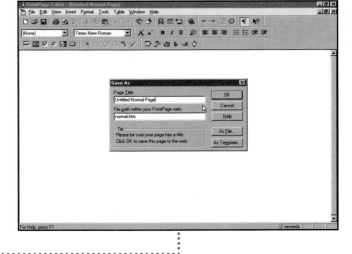

Missing Link

The Page Title and file name supplied by FrontPage are unsuitable. If you leave the file name as normal.htm, you'll have to change the name of the next Normal page—you can't have two files named normal.htm in the same Web folder.

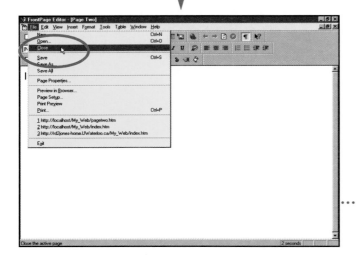

6 When you're finished editing the page, you close it by clicking **File** on the menu bar, then clicking **Close** on the file menu.

Task 3: Creating a Blank Web Page with FrontPage Editor

7 To open an existing page for more editing, click **File** on the menu bar. Then click **Open** to make the Open File dialog box appear. You'll see two tabbed sheets— "Current FrontPage Web" and "Other Location." Click the Current FrontPage Web tab to put that sheet on top. Click the name of the file you want, then click **OK** to open the page and start making your changes. ■

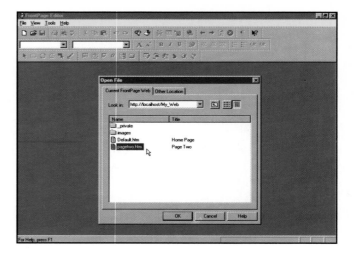

Missing Link

You can create several Webs on each server. FrontPage 97 currently limits the number of Webs to ten per server.

TASK **4**

Creating a Web from a Template

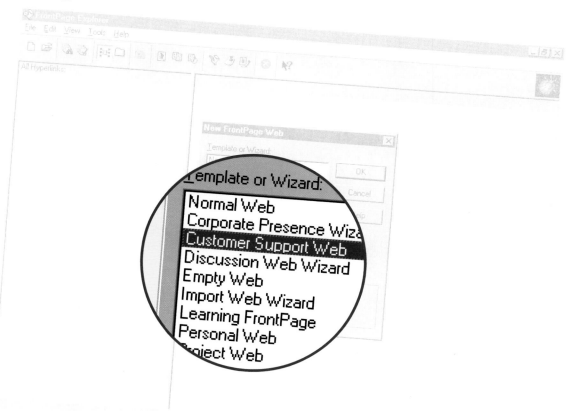

"Why would I do this?"

Templates and wizards are patterns supplied by FrontPage to make your life as a Webmaster easier. Actually, the Normal Web you used in Task 2 was a template, if a very basic one. Templates help you set up a basic format for a Web, which you can then customize according to your tastes and needs. The problem is they don't provide much individuality. However, those that come with FrontPage are enough to get you off to a good start, and some tinkering and creativity will give your Web a character you can call your own.

Task 4: Creating a Web from a Template

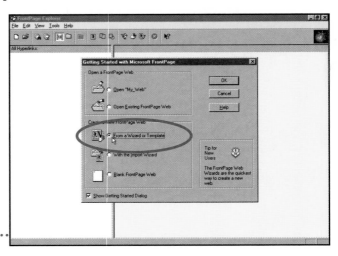

1 To create a Web from a template, start FrontPage to open the Getting Started with Microsoft FrontPage dialog box. Look for the radio button labeled "From a Wizard or Template" and click the button to mark it. Then click **OK**. This opens the New FrontPage Web dialog box.

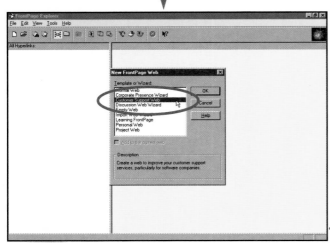

2 For this example, we'll use the Customer Support Web template. But, the same procedure works for all the templates. In the Template or Wizard list box, click **Customer Support Web** to select it. Then click **OK**.

3 When the Customer Support Web Template dialog box appears, type a name for the new Web into the Name of New FrontPage Web text box, then click **OK**. (You can leave the entry in the Web Server or File Location box as it is). FrontPage Explorer automatically creates the Web for you and displays its structure. ■

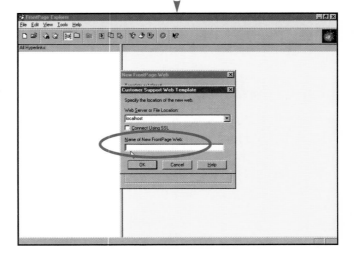

Puzzled?

What are these wizards that appear in the same list box as the templates? Well, they're interactive programs that take information from you and then build a Web based on these specifications. You'll learn more about wizards in Task 5.

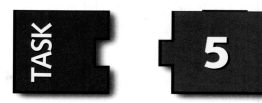

Creating a Web from a Wizard

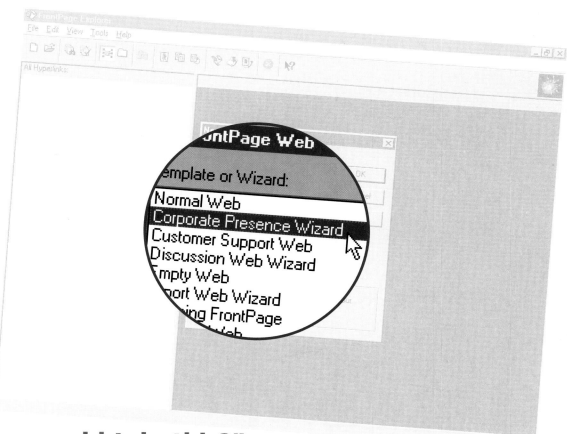

"Why would I do this?"

Like templates, Web wizards help you create Webs according to a predefined structure. Unlike templates, they're more flexible, because they're interactive. Because of this you can customize the end results somewhat, although you're still restricted to the general form provided by the wizard. They're especially useful for setting up moderately complex Webs in a hurry. FrontPage supplies you with a Corporate Presence Wizard and a Discussion Web Wizard.

Task 5: Creating a Web from a Wizard

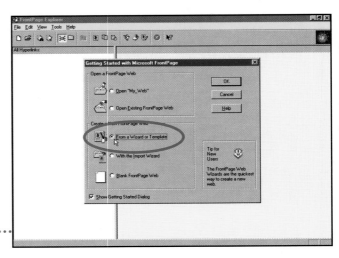

1 To create a Web from a Wizard, start FrontPage to open the Getting Started with Microsoft FrontPage dialog box. Look for the radio button labeled "From a Wizard or Template" and click the button to mark it. Then click **OK**. This opens the New FrontPage Web dialog box.

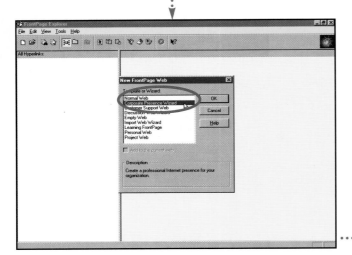

2 For this example, we'll use the Corporate Presence Web Wizard, but the procedure for all Wizards is similar. In the Template or Wizard list box, click **Corporate Presence Wizard** to select it. Then click **OK**.

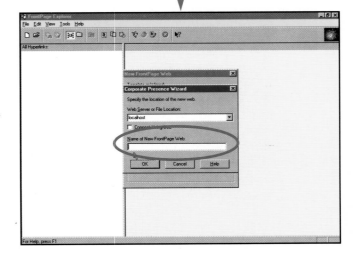

3 When the **Corporate Presence Web Wizard** dialog box appears, type a name for the new Web into the Name of New FrontPage Web text box, then click **OK**. (You can leave the entry in the Web Server or File Location box as it is). When the next dialog box of the Corporate Presence Web Wizard appears, click its **Next** button to move on.

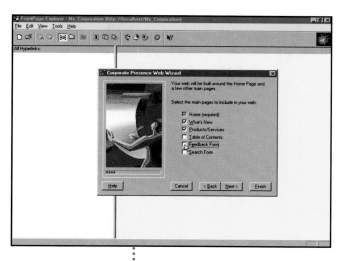

4 Look at the small white boxes in this next dialog box. You use these "check boxes" to pick which pages you want in your Web. A check in a box means that kind of page will be created by the wizard. To put a checkmark in a box, you click it; to erase the checkmark, you also click it. For our example, leave the "What's New" check box checked, and click the "Products/Services" check box to mark it as selected. Finally, click the "Feedback Form" check box to erase the check (we don't want a feedback form). Then click **Next**.

5 The next dialog box gives you some opportunities to tell your visitor about your company. Make any changes you wish, and move on by clicking **Next**.

Puzzled?

If you change your mind about something you did earlier in a wizard, click **Back** until you reach the problem spot.

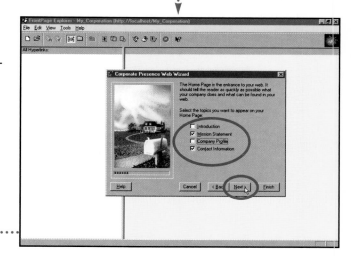

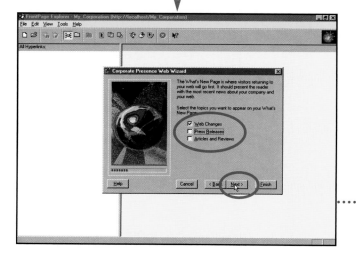

6 In this dialog box, you get a chance to tell your visitors what's new about your company and your Web site. Make any changes you wish, and move on by clicking **Next**.

7 In this dialog box, you get to choose how many products and/or services you want to showcase. Change them if you like, by typing a number into the small text boxes, and click **Next** to go on.

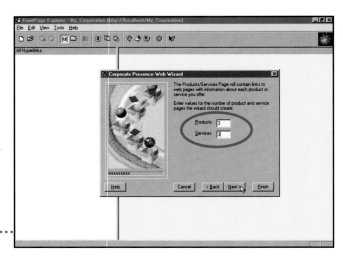

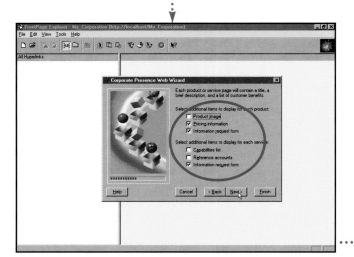

8 The next dialog box helps you set up the descriptive pages for each product or service. Modify them if you wish, and click **Next**.

9 Here you set up a general appearance for your pages. This helps give your Web a consistent "look" that is suitable to your company's products and/or services. Make any changes you like, and click **Next** to go on.

Puzzled?

If you decide you don't need to go all the way through the wizard to get the results you need, click **Finish**. FrontPage Explorer will create the Web by using the information you've supplied to this point.

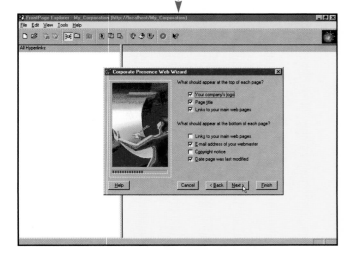

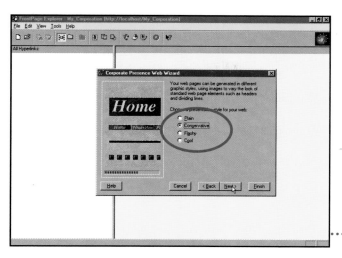

10 The next dialog box lets you choose a graphic style for your pages, ranging from flashy to conservative. Decide what sort of Web you have, and click **Next**.

11 We're getting close! This dialog box helps you choose a color scheme for your Web. Try to keep your colors in tune with the style you selected in Step 10. Then click **Next**.

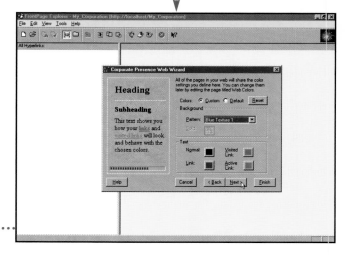

12 Here you decide whether you want "Under Construction" signs on your unfinished pages. Some people disagree with these, feeling that a page shouldn't be on a Web until it's finished, but the choice is yours. Mark the appropriate radio button, and click **Next**.

Task 5: Creating a Web from a Wizard

13 Finally, you get to type the name and address of your Web into the text boxes in this dialog box. Do so, and click **Next**.

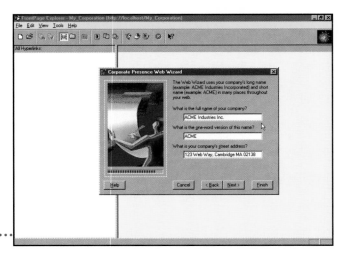

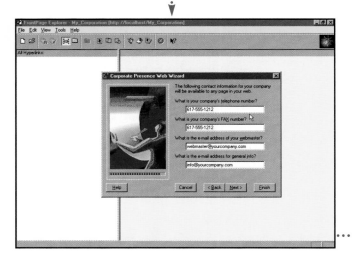

14 Here's where you add your contact information for phone, fax, and e-mail. Type the information into the dialog boxes, and click **Next**.

15 FrontPage can give you a to-do list of tasks required to complete the Web. You'll learn more about this in Task 61. For this example, click the check box to clear it (we don't want a to-do list). Now, believe it or not, you're finished! To prove it, click **Finish** and FrontPage Explorer will create the Corporate Presence Web for you. Now, you can use FrontPage Editor to open the pages and make them look exactly as you want them. ■

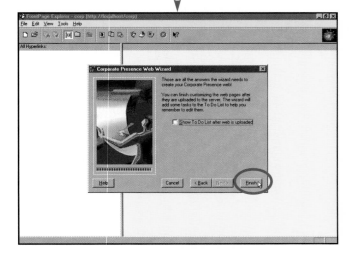

Creating a Web Page from a Template

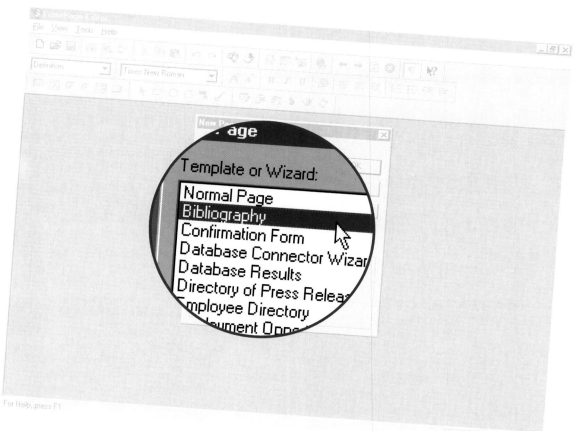

"Why would I do this?"

You've likely discovered, if you have traveled the World Wide Web at all, that certain page styles and formats are repeated from site to site. These guest books, glossaries, bibliographies, and the like, are so common that a standardized approach isn't only possible but desirable. Using these standard formats saves you time and energy, though—as with Web templates—there's a certain cost in individuality. Nevertheless, you'll certainly find uses for the page templates provided with FrontPage 97.

Task 6: Creating a Web Page from a Template

1 Start FrontPage and open FrontPage Editor. Click **File** on the menu bar and then click **New** to open the New Page dialog box. Then use the scroll bar at the right of the Template or Wizard list box to look for the template you want. Click **OK**.

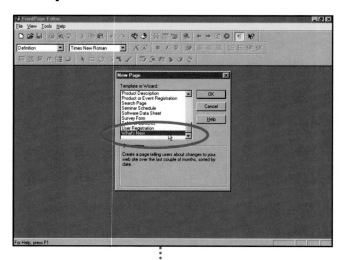

Missing Link

The purple text in some templates is Comment text, and the robot-shaped cursor that appears over it is a Comment WebBot, a special feature of FrontPage.

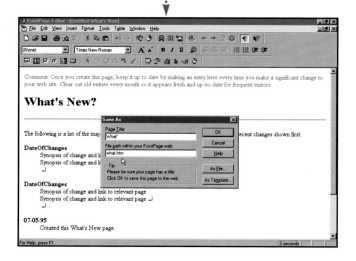

2 Save the page with an informative Page Title and file name. To do this, click **File** on the menu bar, then click **Save As** to open the Save As dialog box. Type the new Page Title into the Page Title text box and the new file name into the File Path Within Your FrontPage Web text box. Don't use the entries that FrontPage supplies— they're too generic. Then click **OK**. Now, you can go ahead and customize your page. ■

Puzzled?

Your page background is likely to be gray, while in the pictures in this book, it's white. No problem—the author's examples were set up this way to make the illustrations reproduce better in the book. You'll learn how to change page color in Task 44.

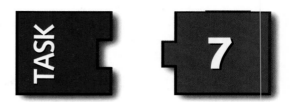

Creating Your Home Page with the Home Page Wizard

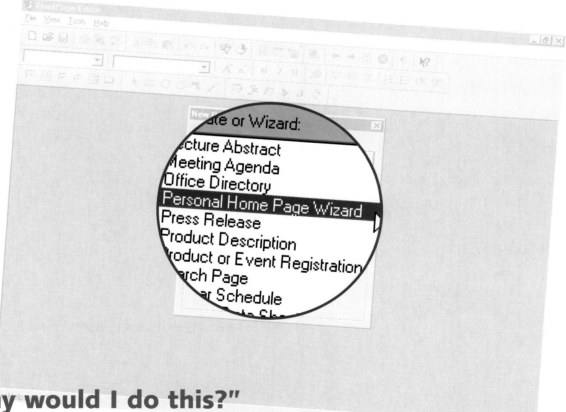

"Why would I do this?"

FrontPage's two Page Wizards—the Form Page Wizard and the Personal Home Page Wizard—are useful for creating pages that are more complex than those provided by the Page Templates. Again, they're time-savers. Since forms are complicated beasts, and outside the scope of this book, we'll work with the Personal Home Page Wizard in this task. Once the Home

Page is in place, you can use FrontPage Editor to create more pages to go with it. We'll assume you've already created a Web where you'll store your Personal Home Page. If you haven't, go to Task 3 and create a Normal Web into which you can put your Personal Home Page.

31

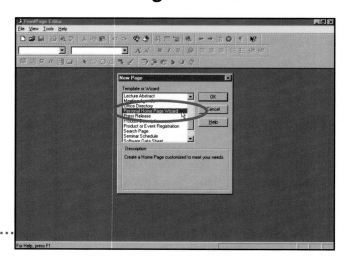

1 Open the Web where you want to store your Personal Home Page. Then start FrontPage Editor. In FrontPage Editor, click **File** on the menu bar and then click **New** to open the New Page dialog box. Then use the scroll bar at the right of the Template or Wizard list box to find the Personal Home Page Wizard. Click it to select it, then click **OK**.

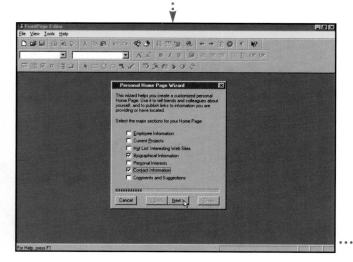

2 When the first Personal Home Page Wizard dialog box opens, click the check boxes to select which items you want the page to include (remember, to erase a check, you also just click it). In the example shown, we're going to include Biographical Information and Contact Information. Then click **Next**.

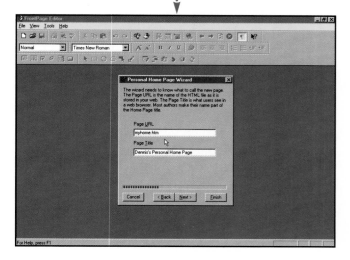

3 In the next dialog box, FrontPage asks you to assign a Page URL (a file name) and a Page Title to your Personal Home Page. It will supply suggestions, but you should change them. Type your new file name into the Page URL text box, and your new Page Title into the Title text box. Then click **Next**.

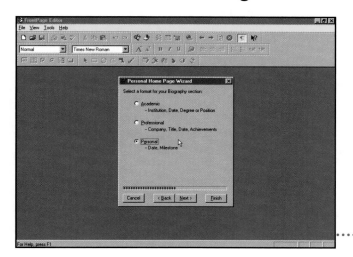

4 In the next dialog box, you mark radio buttons to choose the format for a Biography section. To mark a button, click it; to unmark it, also click it. Then click **Next**.

5 The next dialog box lets you enter your Contact information. You can choose which types of contact to put on the page by clicking in the check boxes to mark or unmark them. Make your choices, then type the information into the text boxes. Then click **Next**.

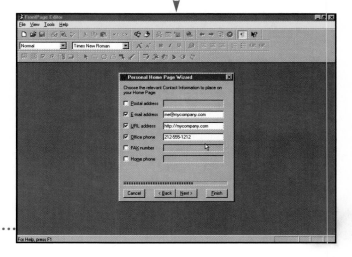

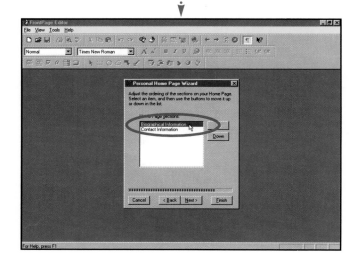

6 Now, you get to rearrange the positioning of your information on your Personal Home Page. Click the item you want to move, then click the **Up** or **Down** buttons to move it. When you're satisfied with the order, click **Next** to go to the last dialog box, where you click **Finish** to create the page. ■

TASK 8

Using FrontPage Explorer's Views

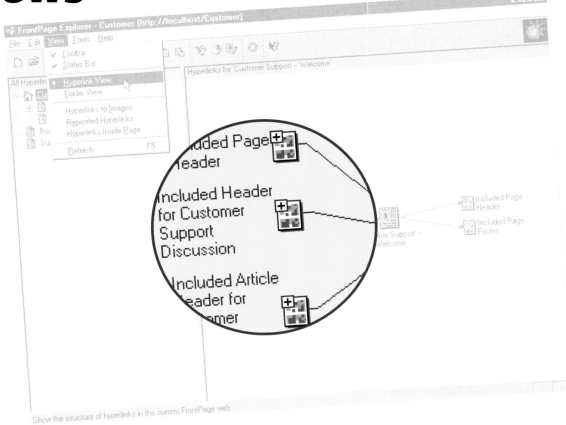

"Why would I do this?"

Webs can become very complex structures. FrontPage Explorer gives you different "Views" of your Web so you can more easily analyze the links among your pages and to the Internet, organize files within Web folders, and generally keep track of things.

To show how Views work, we need a Web with multiple pages. Prepare by creating a Customer Support Web (as in Task 4). If you've already done this, just open the Customer Support Web.

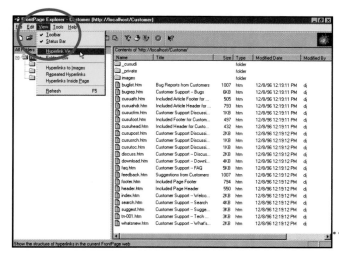

1 FrontPage Explorer has two views, Hyperlink View and Folder View. You can switch between them by clicking **View** on the menu bar, then clicking the name of the View you want when the View menu appears.

2 In the View menu, click **Hyperlink View** to make this View appear in FrontPage Explorer. In the left pane of the window you see icons for all pages and links in the open Web. If you click a page icon in the left pane, that page's icon shifts to the center of the right pane. The lines between pages in the right pane represent links between pages. If a line is broken, the link is faulty.

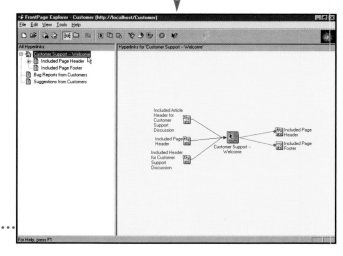

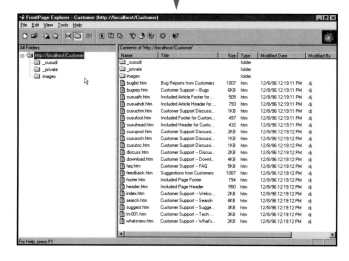

3 Click **View** on the menu bar, then click **Folder View** in the View menu. You can adjust the relative sizes of the panes by dragging the vertical bar that separates them. As in Windows Explorer, you can drag and drop files and folders. ∎

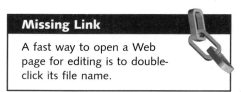

Missing Link

A fast way to open a Web page for editing is to double-click its file name.

Changing Page Titles

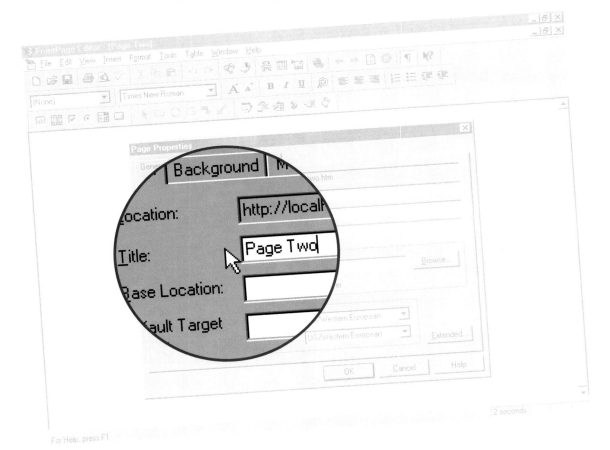

"Why would I do this?"

Page Titles are very important on the Word Wide Web. That's because they appear in the title bar of a browser, and a meaningless one isn't much help to a visitor. Giving useful titles to pages also helps you manage your Web site as it grows.

Remember the Page Title is distinct from the page's file name, though it's convenient if you can make them resemble each other somewhat. As a general rule, don't accept FrontPage's suggestions for file names or Page Titles—they're too generic to be very useful. Keep your Page Titles to 65 characters or less, so they'll fit most browsers.

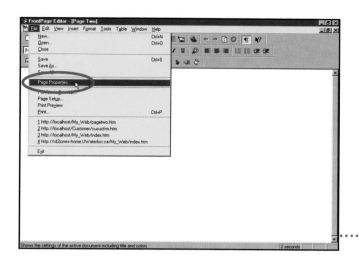

1 In FrontPage Editor, open the page whose title you want to change. Click **File** on the menu bar, then click **Page Properties**.

2 In the Page Properties dialog box, click in the Title text box. Use the Back Space and/or Delete keys to delete the old Page Title, then type a new one. Then click **OK**.

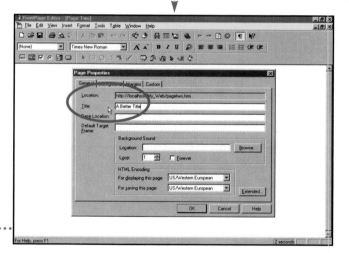

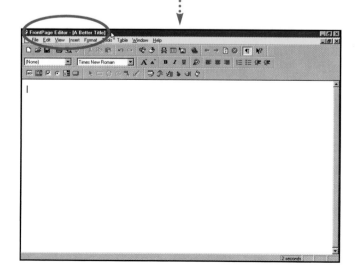

3 Look in the title bar of FrontPage Editor. You'll see the new Page Title there. Now save the page by clicking **File** on the menu bar, then clicking **Save**. ■

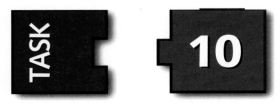

TASK 10

Using the Root Web

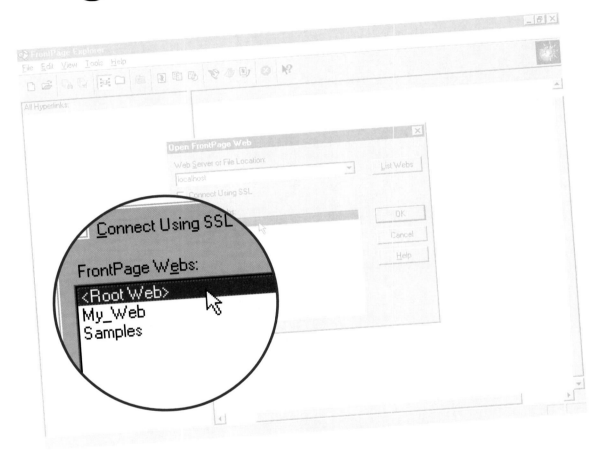

"Why would I do this?"

When you looked at the Open FrontPage Web dialog box, you may have noticed a Web you didn't create—<Root Web>. This was set up when you installed FrontPage, and you shouldn't delete it.

You can use the <Root Web> as your main Web on your Microsoft Personal Web Server. If you do this, the Web will show up in a browser when the user types just your server address into the browser's location text box. The user doesn't have to know the name of the Web itself. Task 10 shows you how to do this.

38

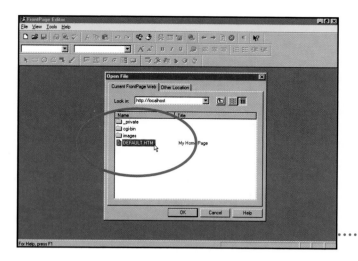

1 Use FrontPage Explorer to open the <Root Web>. Start FrontPage Editor, then click **File** on the menu bar. Click **Open** to reveal the Open File dialog box, and click the Current FrontPage Web tab if that sheet isn't already on top. Click **DEFAULT.HTM** to select the file, then click **OK**.

2 The "generic" Microsoft Personal Web Server's home page appears. You can now delete all the text and pictures on this page and replace them with your own. To remove the unwanted page content, click **Edit** on the menu bar. Then click **Select All** on the Edit menu. The page will now look like a photographic negative, white on black. Now press the Delete key to erase everything on the page. Put your own information on the page, and save it. ■

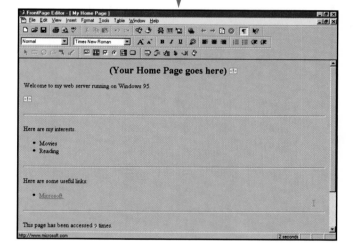

Missing Link

You may already have created a Home Page in another Web. To easily get it into the Root Web, use FrontPage Explorer's Import command. (The Import command works with page files, as well as images.) All your Webs are stored in subfolders in the C:\Webshare\wwwroot folder, so look there to find the name of the Web that contains the Home Page you want to import.

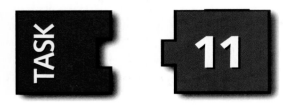

Previewing Your Web Page in a Browser

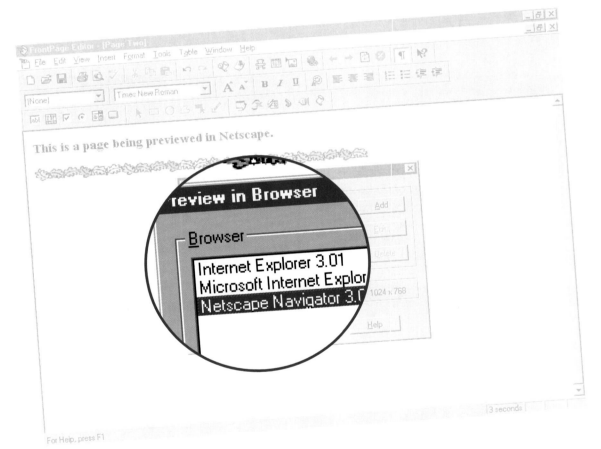

"Why would I do this?"

Since you're working with FrontPage, you likely have a Web browser on your PC. When you installed FrontPage 97, the installation sniffed it out and made it available for previewing purposes. This is important, because FrontPage Editor, while its display is pretty accurate, isn't fully "what you see is what you get." You should always preview your pages to make sure your visitors will see what you want them to.

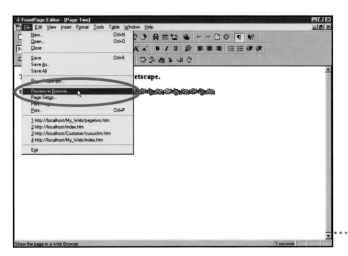

1 To preview a page, first open the page in FrontPage Editor. Then click **File** on the menu bar, and click **Preview in Browser** on the File menu.

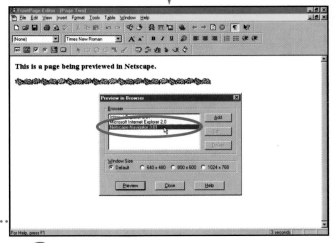

2 When the Preview in Browser dialog box appears, choose the browser you want to use by clicking its name in the Browser list box. Then click **Preview**.

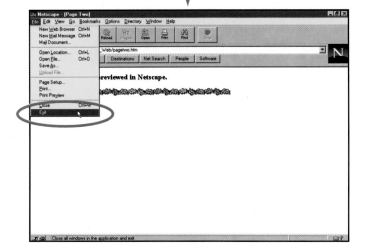

3 FrontPage Editor saves the page automatically, so the browser can load it. The browser starts, and shows you the page. Now you can see whether it looks right, or if you need to make more changes. To return to FrontPage Editor, click **File** on the browser's menu bar, then click **Exit** on the file menu. ■

Missing Link

If you had more than one browser installed on your PC when you installed FrontPage, you can use them all for previewing. It's a good idea to check your pages in all the major browsers, which as of late 1996 were Microsoft Internet Explorer 3.01, and Netscape Navigator 3.01.

41

Viewing Your Web over the Internet

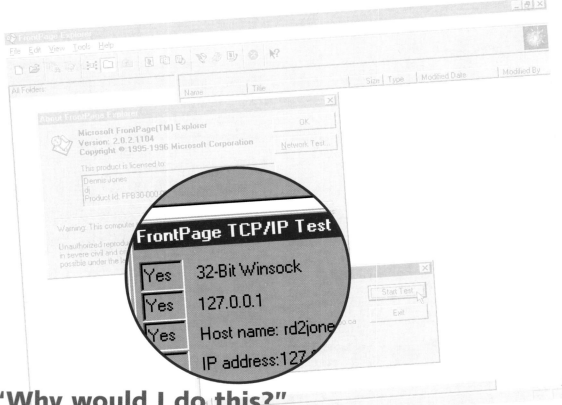

"Why would I do this?"

The bane of Web pages is being slow to appear in a browser. People don't like waiting to see a page, and they'll move on if nothing happens for more than about 15 seconds. While previewing pages in FrontPage Editor is good for checking design, the pages will appear very quickly because they're right there on your PC.

To find out for sure how slowly or quickly your pages appear in a browser, you ought to check them through a real Internet connection. FrontPage Editor shows the projected download time of the page at the right end of its status bar (the bar at the bottom of its window) but this is only a rough guide.

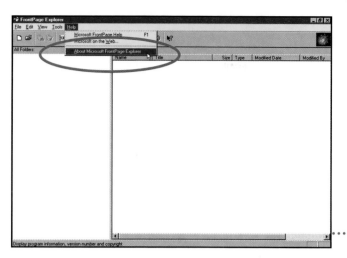

1 Start FrontPage. When FrontPage Explorer loads, slide the mouse to the Getting Started with Microsoft FrontPage dialog box and click **Cancel** to close the dialog box. Click **Help** on the menu bar, then click **About FrontPage Explorer** on the Help menu.

2 In the About FrontPage Explorer dialog box, click **Network Test**. Then, in the FrontPage TCP/IP Network Test dialog box, click **Start Test**. Take a piece of paper and write down the Internet address that appears next to "Host Name:". Duplicate the capitals and small letters exactly. In the example, **rd2jones-home. UWaterloo.ca** would be written down. (Your address will be different.) Then click **Exit**, then in the About FrontPage Explorer dialog box click **OK**. Now you can close FrontPage Explorer; your Webs are accessible even if it's not running.

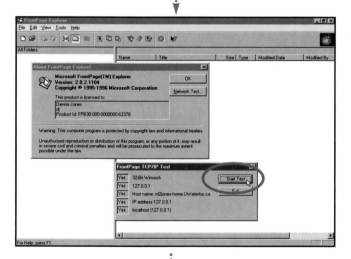

3 Use your Windows 95 Dial-Up connection to connect to the Internet. Now, you and other people can access your FrontPage Webs through the Internet.

Missing Link

Your desktop PC isn't suited to making your Web available to the world. You arrange with your Internet Service Provider to "host" your Web on its machinery. This Task is intended mainly to test your Web.

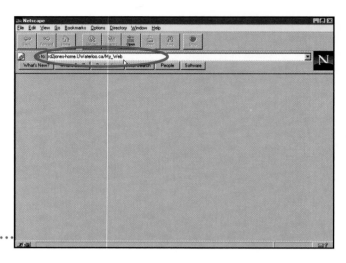

4 Start a browser like Netscape Navigator or Microsoft Internet Explorer. In the browser's location text box, type the address you wrote down in Step 2. Duplicate it exactly. Type a forward slash (/) right after the last letter, and then the name of the Web you want to look at. Then press Enter.

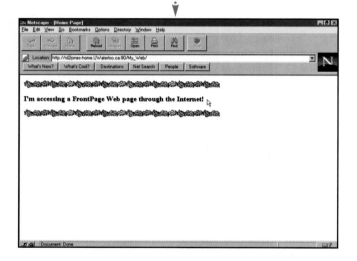

5 A page from your site should appear in your browser window. (If it doesn't, check your spelling and make sure your Internet connection is working.) This page is the one that appears in FrontPage Explorer's Folder View with the file name **Default. htm**. If you have to wait a long time for this or any page to appear (20 seconds, or thereabouts) you should consider redesigning it. The problem is often a large graphic or too many graphics, or big sound files. ■

Puzzled?

If you look at the Location box after your browser opens the page, you'll see the address has changed slightly. An **http//** has been stuck on the front, and there may be an :80 added. This is just the browser and FrontPage going about their business.

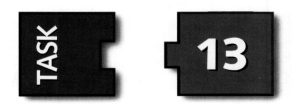

Deleting a Web or a Web Page

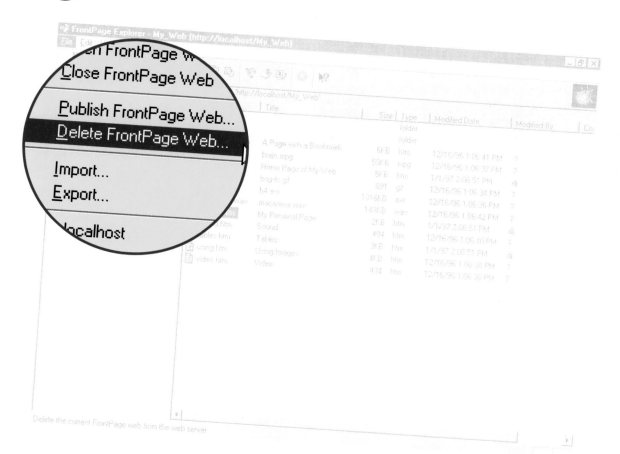

"Why would I do this?"

There are any number of reasons to remove pages from Webs. They might be obsolete, or just pages you've been trying things out in. It's important, by the way, to keep your pages up to date; if you don't, people will see your Web site as a "stale site."

Webs get deleted less often (unless you're experimenting!). Sometimes, they're set up for a temporary purpose, and when that's over, they're erased. Whatever the reasons, deleting either Webs or Web pages is done in FrontPage Explorer.

Task 13: Deleting a Web or a Web Page

1 To delete a Web page, open the Web that contains it. Select Folder View. Then, in the right pane of the FrontPage Explorer window, find the file name of the page you want to delete. Click the file name to select it.

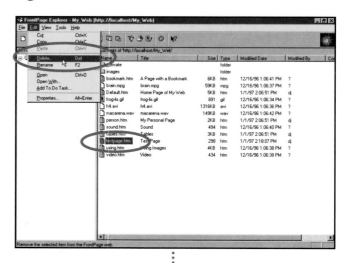

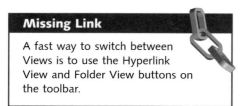

Missing Link

A fast way to switch between Views is to use the Hyperlink View and Folder View buttons on the toolbar.

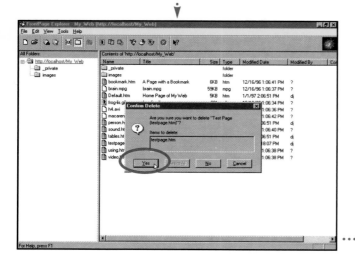

2 Open the **Edit** menu and click the **Delete** option. You'll see a Confirm Delete dialog box. If you really want to delete the page from the Web, click **Yes**; otherwise, click **Cancel**.

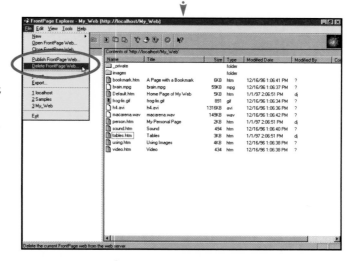

3 Deleting a whole Web is so simple it's a bit dangerous. Open the Web you want to get rid of. Then, open the **File** menu and click the **Delete FrontPage Web** option.

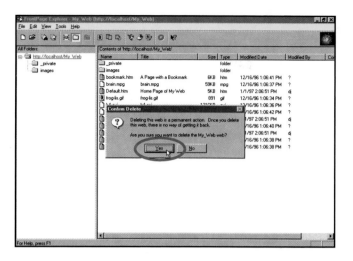

4 In the Confirm Delete dialog box, click **Yes** to erase the Web from your hard disk. If you change your mind, click **No**. Be really sure what you want to do—once you click Yes, the Web is gone forever! In case you were wondering, you don't have to delete all the Web's pages before deleting the Web itself. ■

Missing Link

Don't delete the page whose file name is Default.htm. Current browsers look for this file name when they go to your Web address, and if they don't find it they substitute a really ugly text display of your Web's structure.

Running the Microsoft Personal Web Server

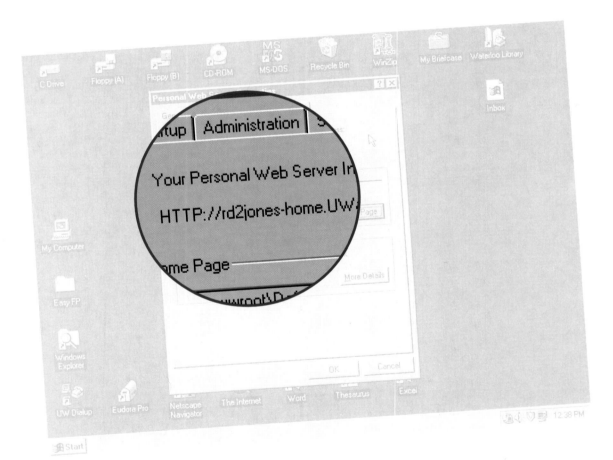

"Why would I do this?"

Assuming you followed Task 1 exactly, you installed the Microsoft Personal Web Server (PWS) when you installed FrontPage. Most of the PWS's operation is in the background, and you won't usually pay much attention to it. However, you may sometimes need to adjust its behavior a little; for example, you may not want it to start running automatically when you start up Windows 95. This task shows you the basics of dealing with the server.

48

1 The Personal Web Server (PWS) starts up with Windows 95. If you don't want to bother switching it off every time you start Windows, double-click **My Computer**, then double-click **Control Panel**, then double-click the **Personal Web Server** icon.

Missing Link

To open the PWS properties dialog box, you can also double-click the PWS icon at the right end of the Windows 95 Taskbar.

2 In the Personal Web Server Properties dialog box, the General sheet will be on top. Click the **Startup** tab to put the Startup sheet on top. To prevent the PWS from running on Windows startup, click in the check box labeled Run the Web Server Automatically at Startup to clear the check box. Next time you shut down and restart Windows, the PWS won't load.

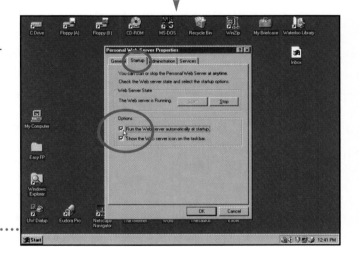

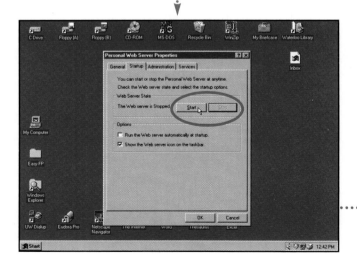

3 Of course, if the server isn't running, you can't use FrontPage Explorer to open Webs. You start (or stop) the server by clicking the **Start** or **Stop** buttons in the Web Server State section of the Startup sheet.

Task 14: Running the Microsoft Personal Web Server

4 The PWS Properties dialog box also provides other server management tools. Click the **General** tab, then click **Display Home Page** to open the <Root Web> home page in a browser window. (For more information on using the <Root Web>, go back to Task 10). Close the browser when you're finished inspecting the page, and you return to the PWS Properties dialog box.

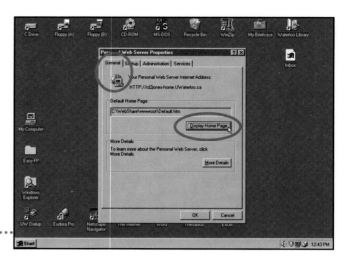

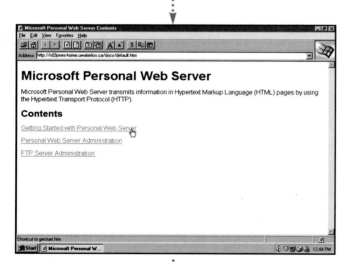

5 The PWS Properties dialog box has other server management tools. Make sure the server is running, then click **More Details**, and a browser window opens showing a table of contents. Click **Getting Started with Personal Web Server** to get instructions on how to test your Internet connection. Clicking **Personal Web Server Administration** gives you information on setting up passwords, user names, and user groups. **FTP Server Administration** helps you set up an FTP service on your PC. When you close the browser, you return to the PWS Properties dialog box.

6 If you need to use FTP services, you need to start the FTP Service of the PWS. Click the Services sheet tab of the PWS Properties dialog box. In the list box, click the FTP entry. Then click the Start button.

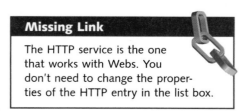

Missing Link

The HTTP service is the one that works with Webs. You don't need to change the properties of the HTTP entry in the list box.

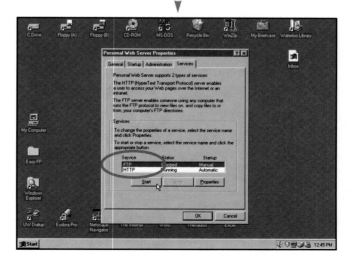

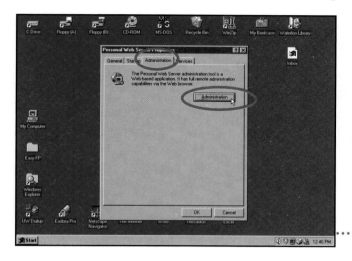

7 To do more elaborate administration, click the **Administration** tab. In the Administration sheet, click **Administration**.

8 In the Internet Services Administrator browser window, you can control several characteristics of the PWS—World Wide Web connections and directories, FTP connections and directories, and local users and user groups. These settings, however, are beyond the scope of this book, so we'll go on now to less complicated tasks. Close the browser to return to the PWS Properties dialog box, and if you're done, click **OK** to preserve any setting changes you made to the server. ■

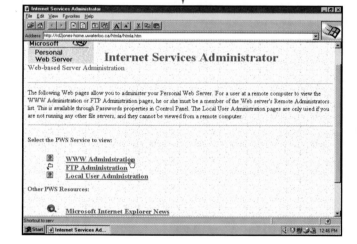

PART II

Working with Text

PART II OF THIS BOOK INTRODUCES you to methods of placing text on your Web pages, and manipulating the text once it's there. You learn how to use the various Web text styles, how to change the appearance of characters, how to lay out text with alignments and indents, how to use lists, and how to use the thesaurus and the spell checker.

But, isn't text getting awfully old-fashioned? If you've spent any time traveling the Web, you'll already know that "multimedia" sites are there in plenty. They're called that because they have blinking headlines, animations, scrolling marquees, background sound, audio players, movie clips, and so on? Don't you have to use all these nowadays to get any attention?

In a word: No. The truth is that most of the useful information in Web sites is textual. Don't forget this if you're new to Web-page design, and if you're feeling that your pages can't be any good if they don't include all the multimedia bells and whistles, dismiss the worry. There are good multimedia sites on the Web, but there are a lot of very bad ones, too. And some of the best and most useful sites hardly use multimedia at all. If you want to get hard information to your users, you will usually end up putting it in text form.

Just as there are design principles that govern the text layout of books or magazines, there are design principles for the text of Web pages. These are pretty straightforward. They're all intended to make it as easy as possible for your visitors to absorb and understand the information you have for them. Here are some basic ones:

- If a page has a lot of text, also use lots of white space. White space is just empty space on a page (on a Web page, it's not necessarily white, but never mind).

- Avoid very long pages that require endless scrolling. Consider breaking the information down into several pages, and linking among them.

- Write clearly and pay close attention to spelling and grammar. Nothing undermines a page's authority as much as confusing language and bad spelling. Even typos suggest the author couldn't be bothered to check his work, and what does that say about the other information he's offering you?

- Remember the title bar that browsers all have? This should have a brief and informative page title. It helps your reader get oriented and stay that way.

- Don't get carried away with fonts. (Fonts are typeface designs and have names like "Times New Roman," "Book Antiqua," and "Garamond." "Bold" and "italic" are not fonts, but attributes of individual characters.) Professional designers never use half a dozen different fonts on a page. Three is enough for most purposes.

- Don't use a lot of capitals. Capitals make a viewer feel that YOU'RE SHOUTING AT HER.

- If you're giving information that lends itself to being presented in point form, consider using bulleted or numbered lists.

- Use horizontal lines economically, usually to separate major blocks of text or to set off a page or section headline.

Finally, the importance of testing can't be emphasized too much. You should especially test your completed pages in different browsers—they may look great in Netscape, but how do they behave in Microsoft Internet Explorer? Always test your pages, and when everything works properly, test them again.

Using Headings

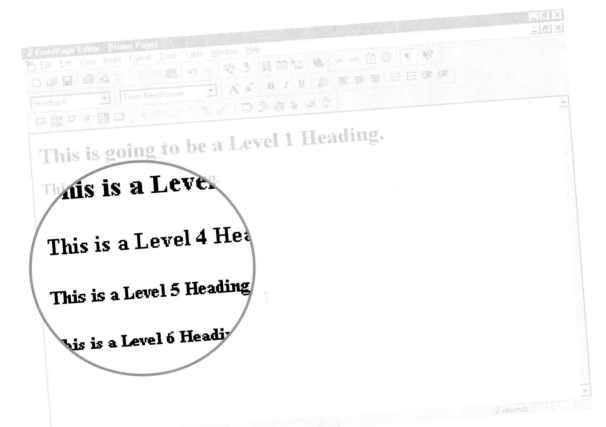

"Why would I do this?"

Headings come in six sizes, and they serve the same purposes as newspaper headlines—their sizes cue the reader to relative levels of importance. In other words, they help you organize the information on a page, and help your visitors understand that organization. They also add some elementary visual interest to a page. Don't over-use them, though—a page full of Level-1 headings makes a visitor feel as if she's being shouted at.

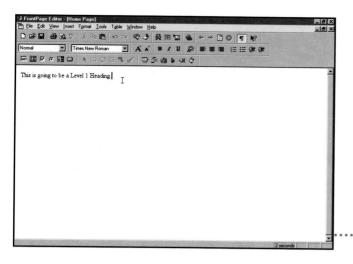

1 Open a Web page in FrontPage Editor. Click once at the place where you want the text of the heading, and then type the heading. Do not press Enter when you're done.

2 Open the **Format** menu, then click **Paragraph**. The Paragraph Properties dialog box appears. In the Paragraph Properties list box, click **Heading 1**, then click **OK**.

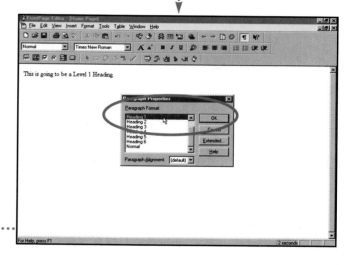

3 Your heading text changes to the largest heading style. Press the **Enter** key to put the insertion point on the next line.

55

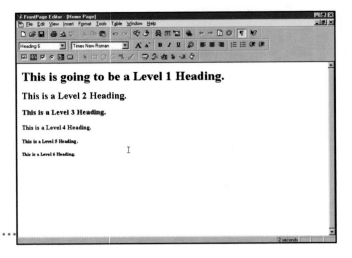

4 To look at the other heading styles, follow steps 1 through 3, each time selecting a different heading size (2 through 6) from the Paragraph Properties list box.

Puzzled?

To delete a heading, select it by double-clicking anywhere on the heading. Then press the **Delete** key.

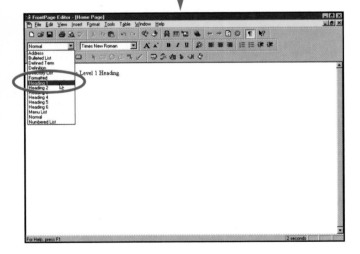

5 There's another way to set heading levels. Carry out Step 1. Then click the down arrow button at the right end of the Change Style box. Click the heading level on the drop-down list to set the new heading level. ■

Missing Link

To change the level of an existing heading, click it anywhere. Then carry out Steps 2 and 3 (or Step 5 by itself).

Adding Normal Text

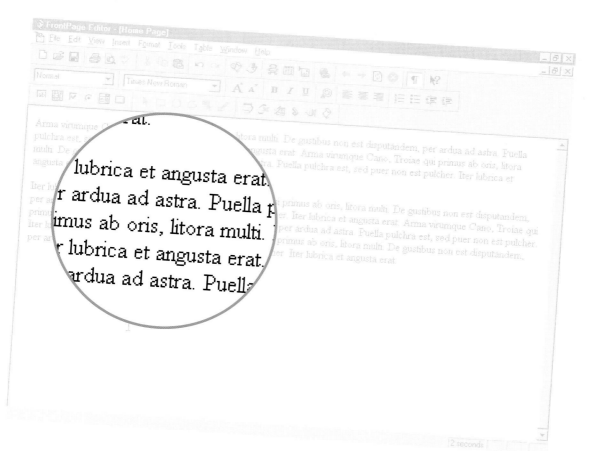

"Why would I do this?"

Despite the graphical nature of the World Wide Web, most of the useful information you find there comes in text form. And most of the text on a Web page is called "Normal" text—this is the text that appears in paragraph bodies. In FrontPage Editor, when you type "Normal" text, it appears automatically in the Times New Roman font. This is referred to as the "default font" for Normal text. However, the font a viewer sees in her browser will vary according to the way the browser's font preference is set.

Task 16: Adding Normal Text

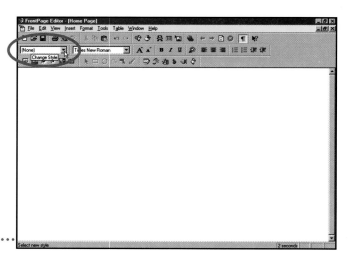

1 Click once at the place where you want the text to begin. Look at the Change Style Box. If it says Normal, you can start typing, pressing **Enter** to end each paragraph. FrontPage Editor automatically adds a space between paragraphs. This is standard. The text remains in Normal style from paragraph to paragraph. If the Change Style box doesn't say Normal, go on to Step 2.

Puzzled?

But, what if you want to break a line early, and have the text continue on the line immediately under it without the spacing you get between paragraphs? To do this, hold down the **Shift** key and press **Enter** once.

2 Click the down arrow button at the right of the Change Style box, and select **Normal** from the drop-down list. Now type your text, pressing **Enter** at the end of each paragraph. ■

Missing Link

You can also select the Normal style by opening the **Format** menu, clicking **Paragraph**, and choosing **Normal** from the Paragraph Properties list box.

Formatting Characters

"Why would I do this?"

The physical appearance of words on a page gives your readers clues about what those words are for, and how important they are relative to everything else. Italics are for emphasis, but also for book titles and certain kinds of citations. Bold is another emphasis, but subtly different from italic. However, don't overdo your use of character formats. If half of your page displays in italic and half in bold, your reader can't tell the difference between what's important and what's really important.

Task 17: Formatting Characters

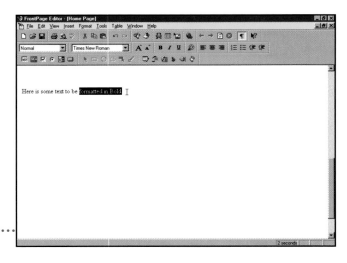

1 Select the piece of text you want to format by dragging across it.

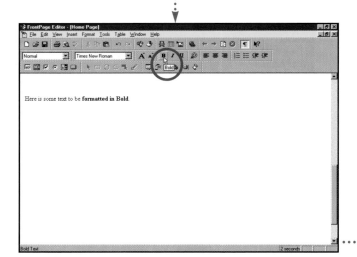

2 To format the selected text as Bold, click the **Bold** button on the toolbar.

3 To format the selected text as Italic, click the **Italic** button on the toolbar.

Missing Link

You can give text more than one format. You can make it bold underlined, bold italic, italic underlined, and so on.

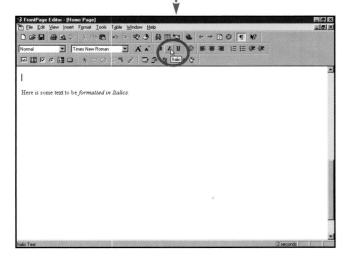

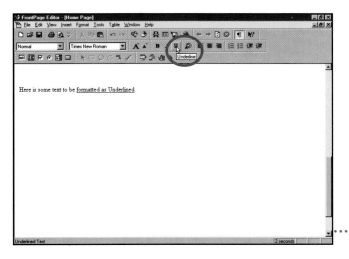

4 To format the selected text as Underlined, click the **Underline** button on the toolbar.

5 To increase the size of the selected text, click the **Increase Text Size** button on the toolbar.

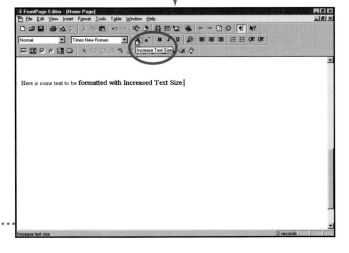

6 To decrease the size of the selected text, click the **Decrease Text Size** button on the toolbar. ■

Puzzled?

To remove character formatting, select the appropriate text. Then open the **Format** menu and click the **Remove Formatting** option.

TASK **18**

Changing Fonts

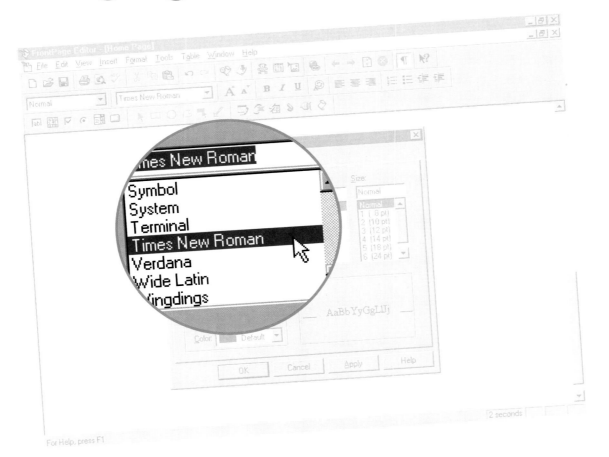

"Why would I do this?"

Using different fonts ("font" refers to what a character looks like) can add enormously to the impact of a page. Fonts do have what you might call (no pun intended) "character"; that is, they suggest a certain mood to the reader.

For example, ornate fonts provide a different atmosphere from that given by a traditional font like Bookman Old Style. However, using a lot of different fonts on one page is bad design. Two, or at the most three, is enough for most purposes.

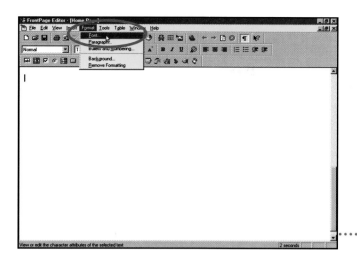

1 Click once at the place where you want the font to start taking effect. Then open the **Format** menu, and click **Font**.

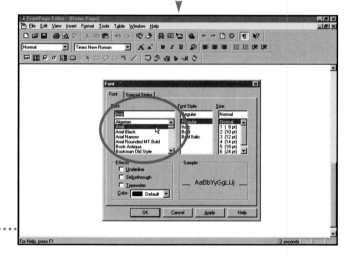

2 The Font dialog box appears. In the Font list box, use the scroll bar to scroll up or down until you see the name of the font you want. Click the font name to select it. The Sample box gives you a preview of its appearance.

3 If you want to change the character formatting, look in the Font Style list box and click **Regular**, **Italic**, **Bold**, or **Bold Italic**.

4 If you want to change the character size, look in the Size box and click the size you want (Normal is the same as Size 3). When you've made all the selections you want, click **OK**. Now, when you start typing, the text will appear in the new font, and in the size and formatting you specified. It will stay that way until you change it again, or until you select Normal from the Change Style box.

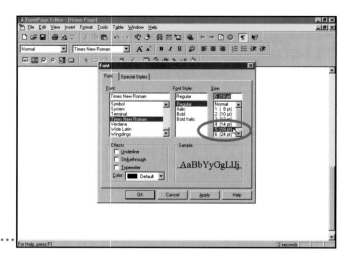

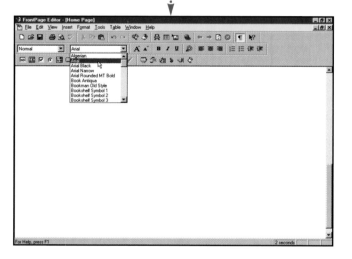

5 A fast way to change the font is to use the Change Font box. Click the arrow button at the right of the box, then click the name of the font you want. ■

Missing Link

To change the font of existing text, first select the text. Then open the **Format** menu, click **Font**, and follow Steps 2 through 4.

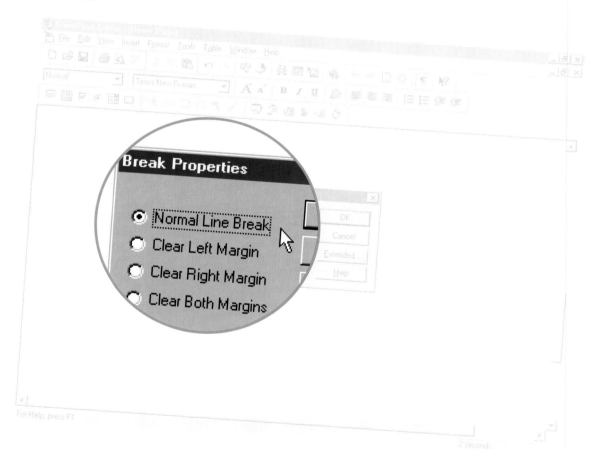

Using Line Breaks

"Why would I do this?"

By now you've noticed that pressing the Enter key at the end of a Normal text paragraph always gives you a blank line before the start of the next paragraph. This may be suitable for most purposes, but suppose you want several short lines of text without spaces between them (such as a quotation). This is where the Line Break comes in.

Task 19: Using Line Breaks

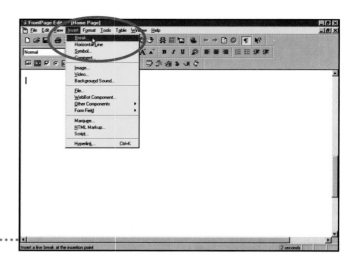

1 Type the first line of the text. Don't press Enter when you reach the end. Instead, open the **Insert** menu and click **Break**.

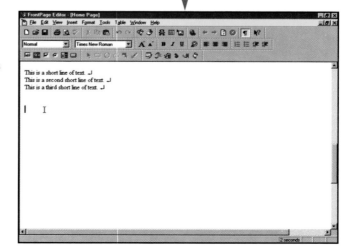

2 In the Break Properties dialog box, mark the radio button labeled Normal Line Break. Click **OK**.

3 You'll see a Line Break symbol at the end of the text line, and the cursor will be at the start of the very next line. Type another line, and repeat Step 2. Do this until you're finished writing the text. Then press **Enter** to make a blank line after the end of the text. ■

Missing Link

You've just learned the slow method. The fast one is to hold down the **Shift** key and press **Enter** once each time you reach the end of the line. This puts a Line Break at the line's end.

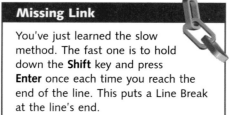

Using Formatted Text

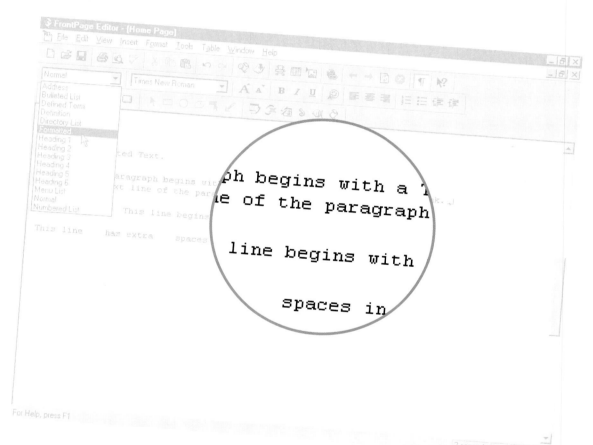

"Why would I do this?"

Why would you use the Formatted style, when you've got that workhorse, Normal? Well, you may need to write text that must have tabs or extra spaces included in it. The Normal style doesn't allow this, but the Formatted style does. You can also use character formatting with it, such as bold, italic, underline, and fonts.

However, test to make sure it looks right in all the common display resolutions. Formatted text doesn't automatically word-wrap in a browser.

A typical use of the Formatted style is with material that needs several levels of indentation or with text that needs various short lines indented.

Task 20: Using Formatted Text

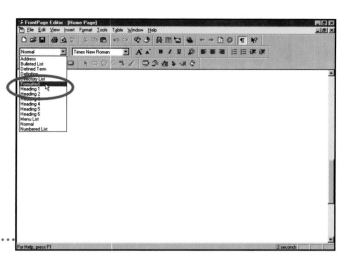

1 Click once at the place where you want the Formatted text to begin. Click the down arrow button at the right of the Change Style box, and click **Formatted** on the drop-down list.

2 Now type your text, using tabs or extra spaces as you need them. With this style you need to end each line manually, because the words don't automatically "wrap" to the next line. To end a line, press the **Enter** key, which puts a blank line on the page before the next line of text starts. If you don't want this blank line, use a Line Break. ■

Missing Link

To change a paragraph of existing text from another style to the Formatted style, click any-where in the paragraph. Then open the Change Style drop-down list, and click **Formatted**. Note the Formatted style affects complete paragraphs.

Using Horizontal lines

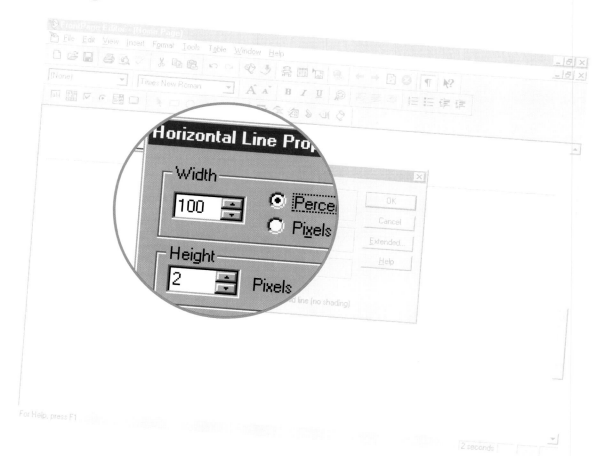

"Why would I do this?"

Paragraphs are units of meaning, and a new paragraph signals the reader that a new unit has begun. However, sometimes you want to announce a more significant shift of emphasis or subject, and for this the horizontal line is effective. These lines are often used with headings, especially to set off the "headline" of a page or to begin a major section within the page.

Task 21: Using Horizontal lines

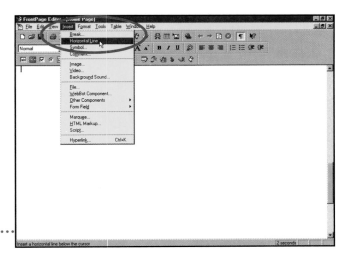

1 Click once at the place where you want the line. Open the **Insert** menu, and click the **Horizontal Line** option. A line appears on the page. This is the "default" line, the one automatically supplied by FrontPage Editor.

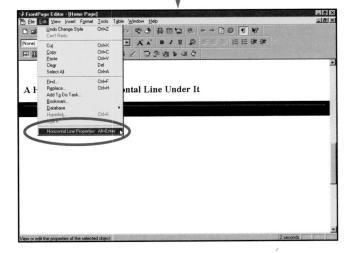

2 To change the line's appearance, click once on it. This selects the line (it becomes white on black).

3 Open the **Edit** menu and click **Horizontal Line Properties**.

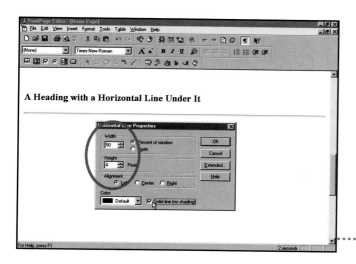

4 In the Horizontal Line Properties dialog box, do this example: type **50** into the Width box, but leave the Percent of Window radio button marked. Type **4** into the Height box. In the Alignment section, mark the **Left** radio button. Click the Solid Line check box to mark it with a check mark.

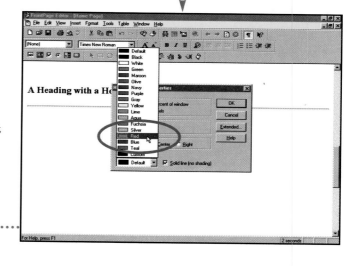

5 To change the color of the line, click the arrow button at the right of the Color box. Click a color on the drop-down list to select it (I chose red). Then click OK.

6 The result is a thick line that's half the width of the page, pushed over to the left margin, and solid red instead of shaded gray. ■

Aligning and Indenting Text

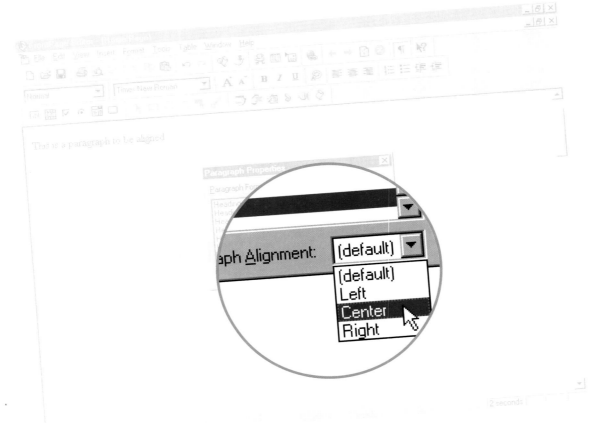

"Why would I do this?"

You'll often want headings or other text to be somewhere other than at the left margin, or indented from both margins. This is a standard operation in page layout, and it's used to help balance the look of text blocks in relation to each other and to pictures on the page. In Front-Page Editor you can "align" text at the left margin, in the center, or at the right margin, as well as indent it.

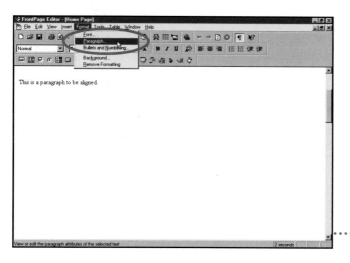

1 Click anywhere in the text you want to align. Open the **Format** menu and click **Paragraph**.

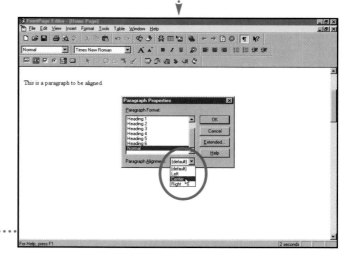

2 In the Paragraph Properties dialog box, click the arrow button at the right of the Paragraph Alignment drop-down list box. Select either **Left**, **Center**, or **Right** ("Default" is the same as "Left") and choose OK.

3 Depending on your choice, the text will be at the left margin, in the page center, or snuggled against the right margin.

73

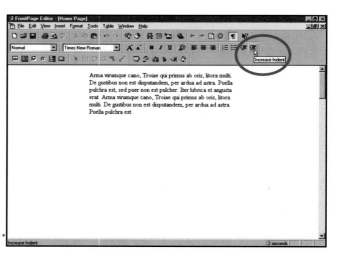

4 You can also indent paragraphs from both margins. To do this, click anywhere inside the paragraph you want to indent. To "squeeze" the paragraph toward the page center, click the **Increase Indent** button on the toolbar. The indent increases each time you click the button.

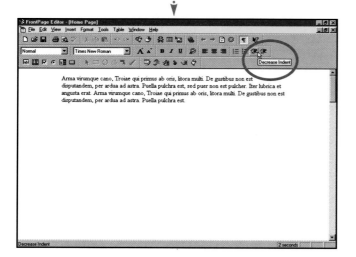

5 To decrease the amount of indenting, click the **Decrease Indent** button on the tool-bar. The indent decreases each time you click the button. ■

Making a Bulleted or Numbered List

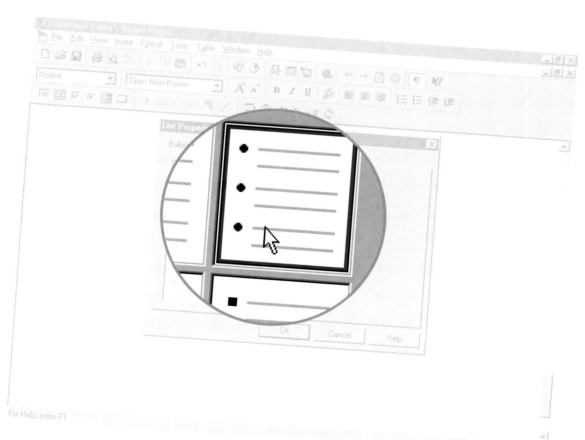

"Why would I do this?"

Lists are excellent for helping you integrate presentation and content in your Web pages. Bulleted lists are for items that require no particular ordering. Numbered lists are used for tables of contents, for establishing a rank order, for a set of instructions, or for any information where relative importance needs to be shown.

Task 23: Making a Bulleted or Numbered List

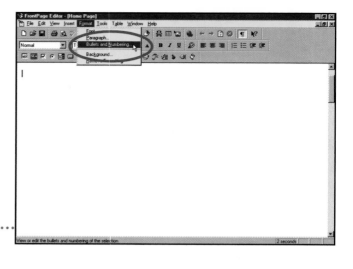

1 Click once at the place on the page where you want the list to start. Open the **Format** menu, and click **Bullets and Numbering**.

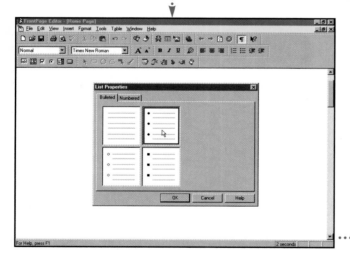

2 The List Properties dialog box has two tabbed sheets. Click the **Bulleted** tab if that sheet isn't on top. Then click the page icon that shows the bullet style you want. Click **OK**, and your first bullet appears on the page.

3 Start typing your list, pressing **Enter** at the end of each item. When you've finished, press **Enter** twice to stop inserting bulleted items.

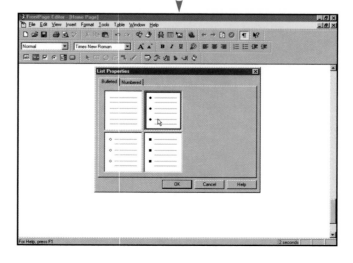

76

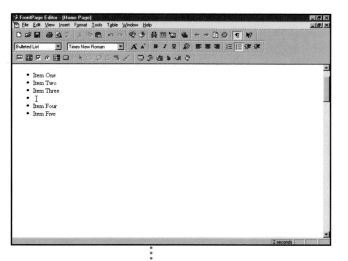

4 To insert an item into an existing list, click immediately to the right of the preceding item, press **Enter**, and type the new item. Then slide the mouse pointer to above or below the list, and click to place the insertion point outside the list.

Puzzled?

To delete an item from a list, drag across it and press the **Delete** key to remove the text. Then press the **Delete** key again. This removes the bullet or number.

5 To make a numbered list, open the List Properties dialog box as you did in Step 1. In that dialog box, click the tab labeled "Numbered." Then click the page icon that shows the numbering style you want. Then click **OK**, and the number 1 appears on the page.

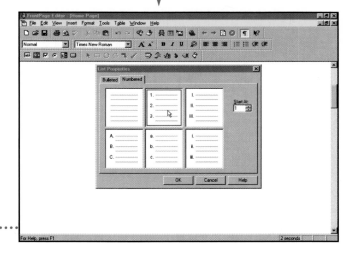

6 Start typing your list, pressing **Enter** at the end of each item. When you've finished, press **Enter** twice to stop inserting numbered items. To insert an item into a numbered list, use the technique in Step 4. Note the numbering is adjusted automatically when you do this. ■

Missing Link

A fast way to turn bullets or numbering on or off is to click the **Bulleted List** and **Numbered List** buttons on the toolbar.

TASK

24

Changing the Style of a List

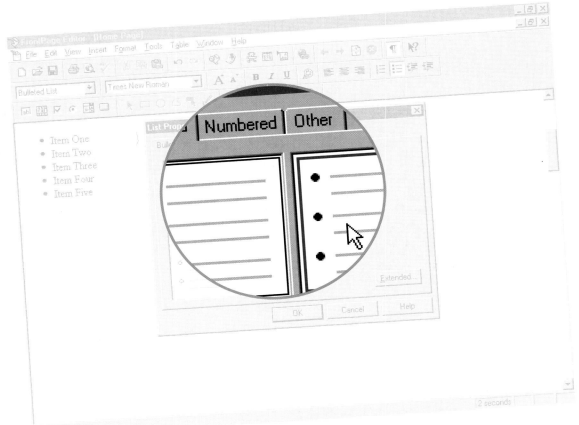

"Why would I do this?"

You may find that your bulleted list really needs to be a numbered one, or vice versa. Or, you may decide the list shouldn't be a list at all, but plain, old Normal text. Fortunately, there's an easy way to make these changes.

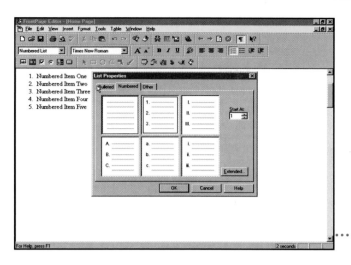

1 To change a numbered list to a bulleted list, begin by clicking anywhere in the numbered list. Then open the **Format** menu and click **Bullets and Numbering**. The List Properties dialog box opens, with the Numbered sheet on top.

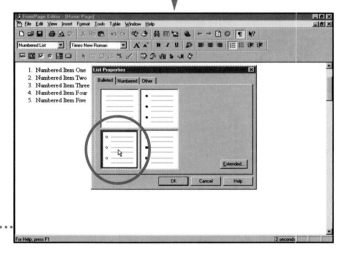

2 Click the **Bulleted** tab to put the Bulleted sheet on top. Click the page icon that shows the bullet style you want.

3 Click **OK**. The numbered list immediately becomes a bulleted list, with the bullet style you selected.

4 To change a bulleted list to a numbered list, click anywhere in the bulleted list, then do Step 1. In the List Properties dialog box, select the **Numbered** tab to put the Numbered sheet on top. Click the page icon that shows the numbering style you want.

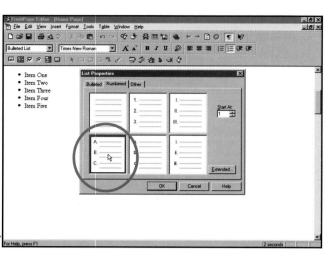

5 Click **OK**. The bulleted list immediately becomes a numbered list, with the numbering style you selected.

6 To turn a list into Normal text, open the List Properties dialog box, just as you've been doing in the preceding steps. Then, in either the Bulleted or the Numbered sheet, click the top-left page icon (it has no bullets or numbers). Then click **OK**, and the list will turn into Normal text. ■

Missing Link

To start a list at a number other than 1, click in the Start At box in the List Properties dialog box and type the starting number you want. Then click **OK**. Of course, you must select the Numbered sheet to choose the page icon with the numbering style you want.

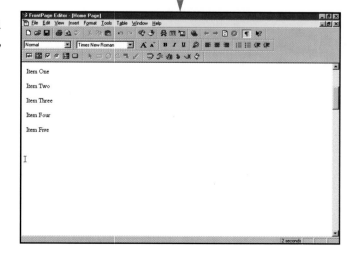

Making a Definition List

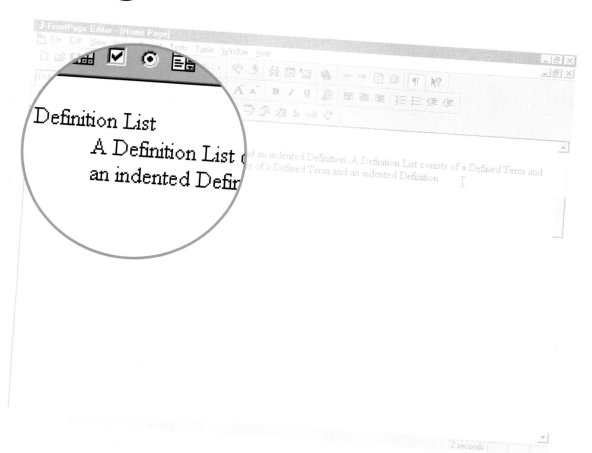

"Why would I do this?"

Sometimes, you need a text layout that is made up of short headings followed by one or more paragraphs. (The most familiar layout of this sort is a dictionary.) Web pages often arrange text like this, using what's called a "definition list." A definition list is a collection of entries, and each entry is made up of a term and its definition. In these lists, the paragraph that gives the definition is automatically indented.

Task 25: Making a Definition List

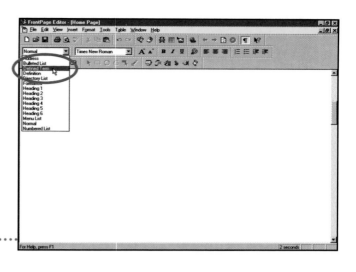

1 Click once at the position where you want the definition list to begin. Then, open the Change Style box, and click **Defined Term**.

2 Type the term to be defined, and press **Enter**. The insertion point moves to the next line, and automatically indents. Now type the definition, and press **Enter** again.

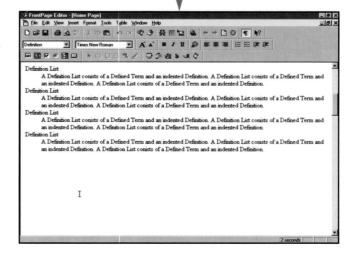

3 Repeat Step 2 until you've finished the list. Then press **Enter** twice to end the list. ■

Missing Link

You can use character formatting in a Definition list. You might want to format the Defined Terms as Bold to make them stand out.

Spell Checking Your Work

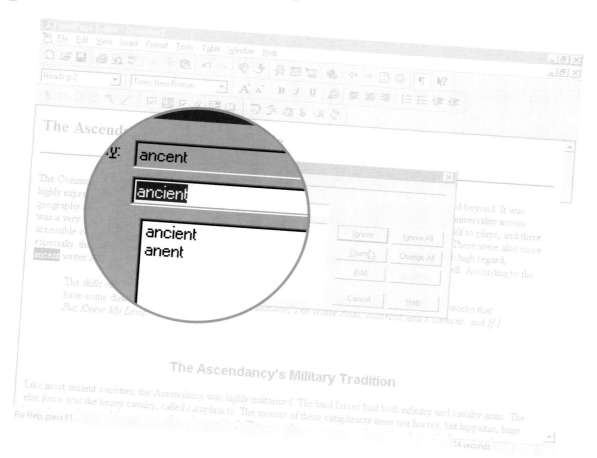

"Why would I do this?"

Many people have difficulty with spelling. But as an author (Web or otherwise) you need to make sure your text isn't riddled with spelling errors. If it is, that suggests you're careless, and your visitors will wonder about the quality of the other information on your site. What it comes down to is this: Bad spelling is unprofessional.

1 To check a page for spelling errors, first open the page in FrontPage Editor. Then open the **Tools** menu and click the **Spelling** option.

2 The Spelling dialog box opens, and the spell checker highlights the first misspelled word it finds. The Change To box shows what the spell checker thinks is the correct spelling. To accept this, click **Change**, and the speller goes on to the next error. If the correct spelling is down in the Suggestions list box instead, click that entry in the list box, and then click **Change**. To correct every occurrence of a particular misspelling on the page, click **Change All**.

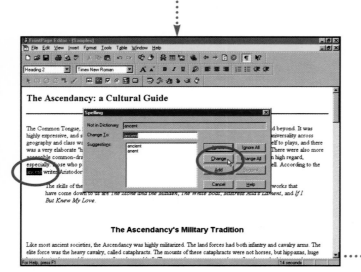

3 The speller may highlight a word you know is correct, and you may want to add it to the speller's dictionary so it won't be tagged as an error again. To do this, click the **Add** button. If the word is correct but you don't want to add it, click **Ignore** to bypass this occurrence of the word and go on to the next misspelling (click **Ignore All** to bypass the word throughout the rest of the page).

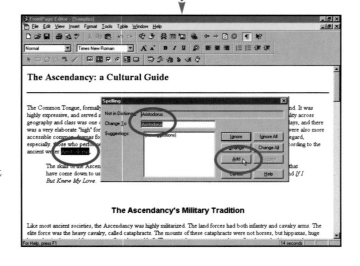

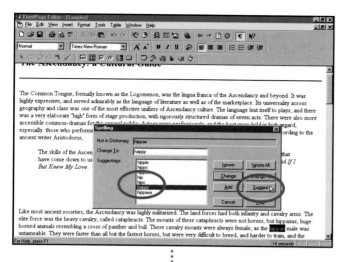

4 If neither the Change To box nor the Suggestions list box shows the correct spelling, you can click one of the entries in the list box and then click **Suggest**, to get a list of words similar in spelling to the incorrect one. If one of these words is right, click it, then click **Change**. If all else fails, click in the Change To text box, type the correct spelling, and then click **Change** to correct the mistake and go on to the next error.

5 When the page has been fully checked, you see a dialog box that says so. Click **OK** to close it and return to FrontPage Editor. ■

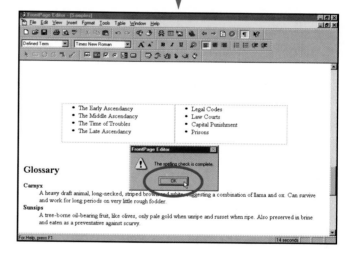

Using the Thesaurus

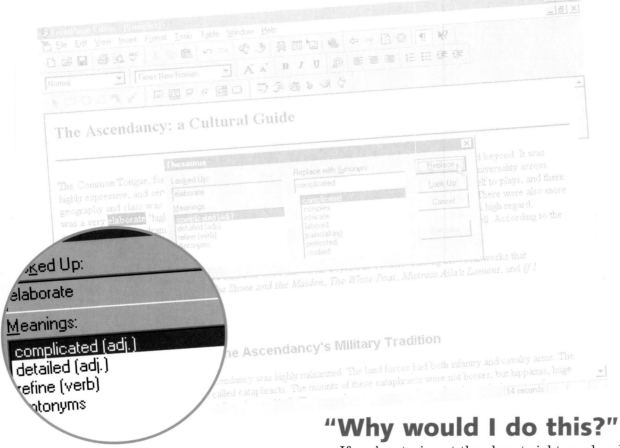

"Why would I do this?"

If you're staring at the almost-right word and can't think of the right one, try using FrontPage Editor's thesaurus to find it. Variety in word choice helps make your writing more vivid and memorable. Don't get infected by "thesaurusitis," though; if you find yourself replacing "appearance" with "semblance" you may be going too far!

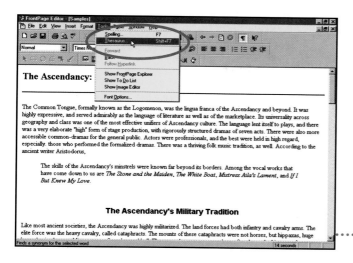

1 Click on the word for which you want a synonym. Then open the **Tools** menu and click **Thesaurus**.

2 The Replace with <u>S</u>ynonym box suggests a word as the replacement. If you like it, choose **Replace**. The dialog box closes, and the original word is automatically replaced with the new one. If the suggested word isn't right, click a better one from the list box under the Replace with Synonym text box, and click **Replace**.

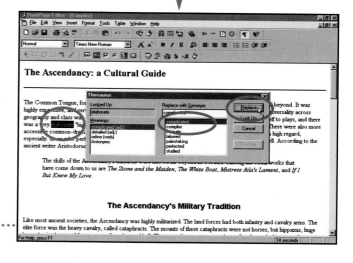

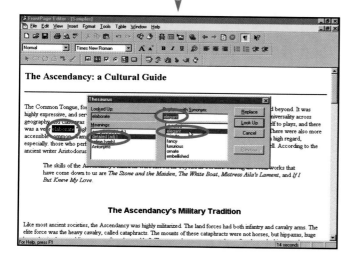

3 If you don't see the right word anywhere, click a similar meaning in the Meanings list box. More words appear in the right-hand list box. Click one of these, then click **Replace**. If these don't satisfy, click any word from either list box, then click **Look Up**. Yet more words appear in the list boxes. (To go back to the previous list, if there is one, click **Previous**.) Click a suitable word, then click **Replace**. ■

Using Find and Replace

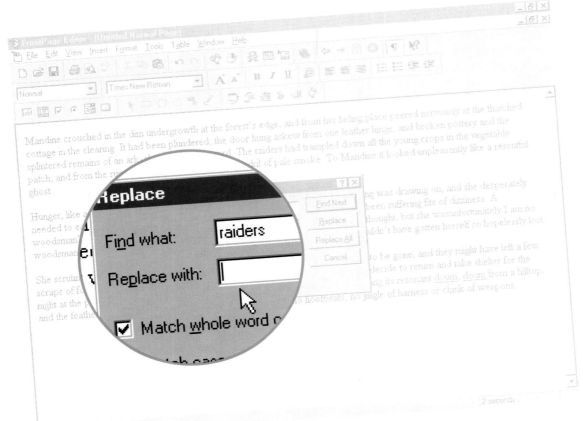

"Why would I do this?"

Sometimes, you want to locate a particular word or phrase that's buried somewhere in the text of your page. To do this, you use FrontPage Editor's Find option. Or, you may want to replace all occurrences of a certain word with a different word. In this case, you use the Replace option. Using either Find or Replace is faster and more trustworthy than scanning the page by eye—you might miss the word, but FrontPage won't.

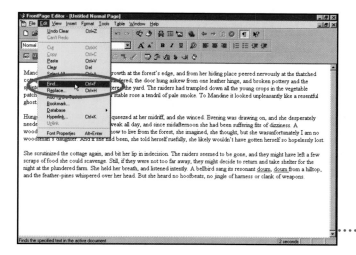

1 To find a word or phrase, click once at the very top of the section in which you want to search. Then open the **Edit** menu and click **Find** to open the Find dialog box.

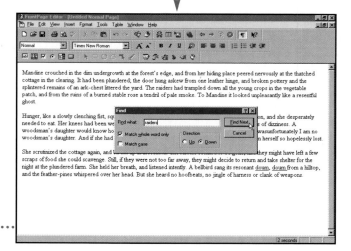

2 Type the text you want to search for into the Find What text box. It's also a good idea to mark the Match Whole Word Only check box. If you don't, and you search for the word **led** for example, the software will find fi**led**, b**led**, and so on. Depending on where you are in the text, you might also mark the Up or Down radio buttons. When you've completed the dialog, click **Find Next**.

3 When FrontPage Editor finds the word or phrase, it stops and highlights the text. In the example, the word "raiders" was searched for, and it was found in the first paragraph. To go on searching for the word, click **Find Next**.

4 When FrontPage Editor reaches the end of the page, it tells you it's finished. Now you can click **OK** to return to the workspace.

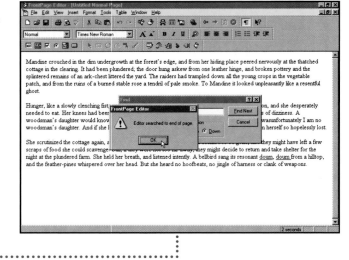

Puzzled?

Unlike the Speller, Find and Replace works downward from the cursor position to the end of the page, and stops there. If you want to do Find or Replace on the entire page, place the insertion point at the very top-left margin of the page. Use the **Ctrl+Home** key combination to do this quickly.

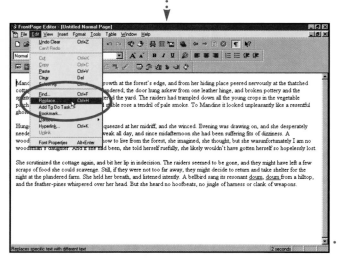

5 To replace a word or phrase, click once at the very top of the section in which you want to do the replacing. Then open the **Edit** menu and click the **Replace** option to open the Replace dialog box.

6 In the Find What text box, type the word or phrase you want to replace. Then type the replacement text into the Replace With text box. Again, it's a good idea to mark the Match Whole Word Only check box. When you've completed the dialog box, click **Find Next**.

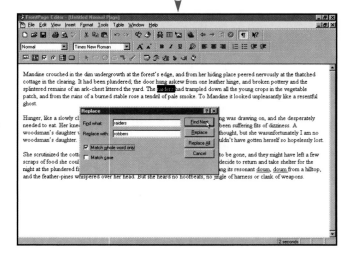

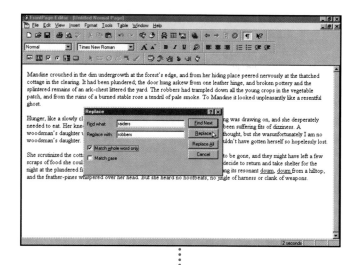

7 When FrontPage Editor finds the word or phrase, it highlights it. If you want to change it, click **Replace**. Then click **Find Next** to go on searching. If you decide to leave this occurrence as it is, just click **Find Next** instead of **Replace**, and it won't be replaced.

Missing Link

If you're very sure about the text you're replacing, click **Replace All** instead of **Find Next**. This automatically replaces every occurrence of the old text with the new text. If you make a terrible mistake, close the Replace dialog box, immediately open the **Edit** menu, and click the **Undo Replace** option.

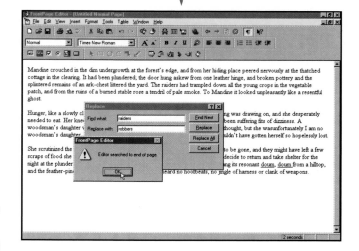

8 When FrontPage Editor reaches the end of the page, it tells you it's finished. Now you can click **OK** to return to the workspace. ■

TASK **29**

Printing Your Pages

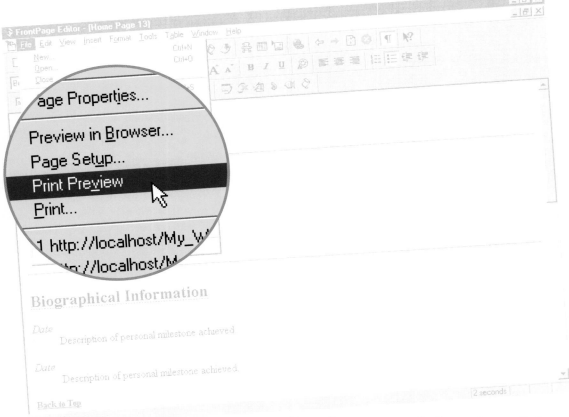

"Why would I do this?"

Printing text-heavy pages in particular is a good idea, since spelling mistakes, typographical errors, and bad grammar seem to stand out better on paper than they do on a screen. (It's a mystery why this is so, but a lot of people find it to be true.) Hard copy also gives you another perspective on your page design, and you can scribble fix-it notes to yourself in the margins!

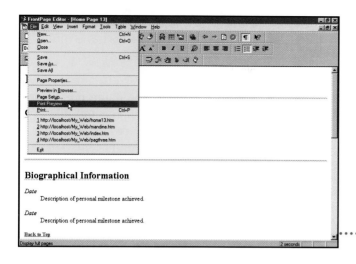

1 You can preview a page before printing it. Open the **File** menu and click the **Print Preview** option.

2 In the Print Preview window, you can click buttons to go to the **Next Page**, to the **Previous Page**, to show **Two Pages** side by side, or **Zoom In** or **Zoom Out**. (Clicking the hourglass cursor anywhere on the page also zooms.) If you like what you see, go ahead and click **Print** on the toolbar. If you want to make changes before printing, click **Close** to return to the FrontPage Editor workspace.

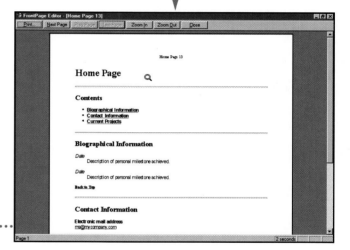

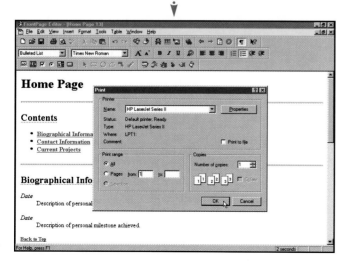

3 If you click **Print**, the Windows 95 Print dialog box opens. Set the print job up the way you want it, then click **OK** to send the page or pages to the printer. (Your Print dialog box will differ from the one shown, depending on what kind of printer is connected to your PC.) ■

Missing Link

You can print from the File menu without going through Print Preview. Open the **File** menu, then click the **Print** option. Or, you can simply click the printer icon on the Standard Toolbar.

PART III

Working with Hyperlinks

PART III OF THIS BOOK SHOWS you how to create, test, and modify hyperlinks within your Web site, and how to link pages of your site to others on the World Wide Web.

Without hyperlinks there would be no World Wide Web. Links are the nervous system of the Web; they connect millions upon millions of pages to make the remarkable universe of information and communication that people call "cyberspace." Somewhat less poetically, *hyperlink* (or "link") generally refers to the highlighted words or specially defined images that you click in a Web page to access a different resource on the Web or the Internet.

Where did all this come from? Well, until a few years ago, the Internet was the domain of scholars and researchers, and few people outside government and research institutions could get at it. In fact, the Internet was around long before the World Wide Web; as late as 1990, in fact, the Web did not yet exist. It might never have come into being, except that Tim Berners-Lee and his team at the European Organization for Nuclear Research (CERN) designed and released a "hypertext" system to permit better communication among researchers in high-energy physics. ("Hypertext" is just text that is interconnected by hyperlinks.) The software was written specifically for the Internet, and was released in 1991. Not long after that, the Internet was made available for public use and the rest, as they say, is history.

The key element that makes Web pages different from printed pages is the existence of these hyperlinks, courtesy of Mr. Berners-Lee. Many of your links will be text links, so this is a good place to mention how to use them to their best advantage.

- When you're choosing which words to use for the link, think about them from your visitors' point of view. It helps if the link itself suggests what happens if you click it. An ambiguous link, which a reader must follow to discover whether he really wants to go there, is a potential waste of time. An ambiguous link says: "Click here to go back;" a clear one says: "To Table of Contents." You can make the purpose of a link even clearer by wording the surrounding text to give it a context.

- Be sure the links on a page behave as you've led the viewer to expect. Also, check your site regularly for broken links. Broken links suggest you don't maintain your pages effectively.

- Include a go-to-home-page link on all your pages. This is especially true if you have a large or complex site.

- On pages more than a couple of screens long, include "Top of Page" links at suitable points. This makes it unnecessary for viewers to scroll and scroll and scroll to return to the page top.

- You may have a set of navigation links at the top of your page (navigation links are links to other main parts of the Web site, or to other sites). If you do, and if the page is more than a couple of screens long, repeat the navigation links at the bottom of the page. Again, this relieves the visitor of a lot of scrolling.

- Text hyperlinks, since they're (usually) colored and underlined, stand out from their background. They drag the reader's eye toward them, and if there are too many of them, their presence can overpower the meaning of the surrounding text. Unless it's a table of contents, your page shouldn't have so many links that it appears to be mostly blue underlining.

Creating a Link

"Why would I do this?"

Links, formally called "hyperlinks," are the highlighted words (or specially defined images) that you click in a Web page to go to another place on the World Wide Web. You need links to connect the pages within your site, so that visitors can move from one page to another. You also use links to connect your own Web site to others on the World Wide Web. In fact, without links there would be no Internet or World Wide Web at all.

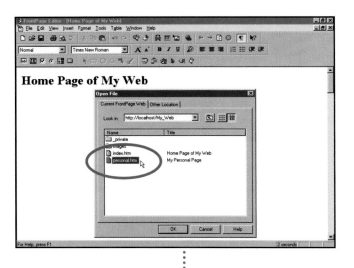

1 Begin by opening two Web pages in FrontPage Editor. Open the **File** menu and click **Open**. When the page appears, open the File menu again and repeat the procedure.

Missing Link

In the Open File dialog box, you can hold down the **CTRL** key and click the names of the pages you want. This selects them, and when you click **OK**, FrontPage Editor opens them.

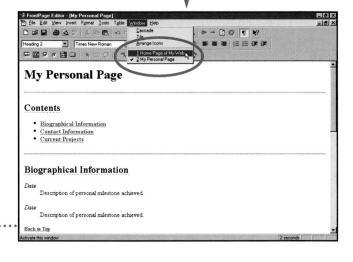

2 Open the **Window** menu and click the name of the page on which you want to create the link. Doing this makes that page the "active page"—that is, the page that's affected by your next actions. As soon as you click its name, it appears in the FrontPage Editor workspace.

3 In the active page, type some text to be the link. Then drag across it to select it.

4 Open the **Edit** menu and click **Hyperlink** to open the Create Hyperlink dialog box.

Missing Link

You can also click the **Create or Edit Link** button on the tool-bar to open the Hyperlink dialog box.

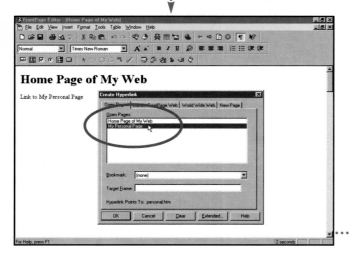

5 In the Create Hyperlink dialog box, if the Open Pages sheet isn't on top, click the **Open Pages** tab. The list box on this sheet displays the Page Titles of all pages currently open in FrontPage Editor. Click the name of the page that you want the visitor to see when he uses the link.

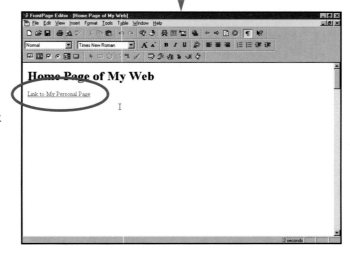

6 Click **OK**. On the page, the link text will be highlighted in black; click once anywhere to remove the highlighting. The link is now set up with the standard blue text and underlining that indicates a link. ■

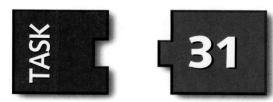

Testing a Link

"Why would I do this?"

Since links are the nervous system of your site, you should make sure they work properly— people really hate to click a link, and then get an error message saying the page isn't available. If your site does too much of this, nobody will hang around for long.

1 You can use FrontPage Editor to test links within a Web stored on your machine. To test a link this way, first click it once. Next, open the **Tools** menu, then click **Follow Hyperlink**. The destination page should appear in the FrontPage Editor workspace.

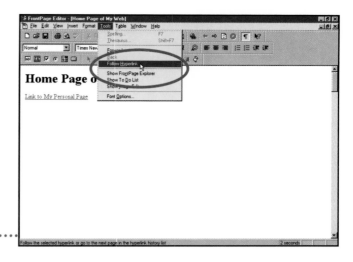

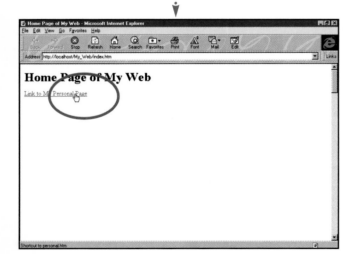

2 For a more "real-world" test of a link within your own site, open the **File** menu and click the **Preview in Browser** option. As you learned to do in Task 3, choose a browser to open the page with the link. When you click the link, the destination page should appear in the browser window. ■

Missing Link

If you slide the cursor over a link while you're in FrontPage Editor, the address of the link's destination page will appear down in the FrontPage Editor's status bar.

Linking to a Bookmark

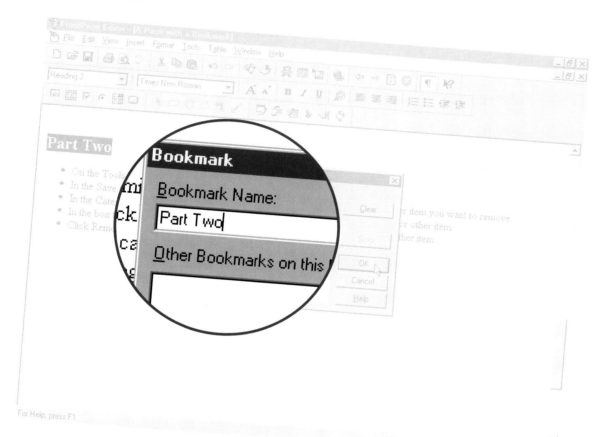

"Why would I do this?"

The linking technique described in Task 30 is somewhat inflexible. If a person clicks such a link, it's always the top of the destination page that appears in her browser window. But, sometimes you don't want the person to have to look at the top of the page—if the page is a long one, the information she's after may be several screens down. To send her directly there, you use what's called a "bookmark." The bookmark is always created on the destination page that the link points to. This destination can be any page in the Web site, including the page where the link itself resides (you use this latter arrangement to take a reader quickly to another part of the page she's currently looking at).

Task 32: Linking to a Bookmark

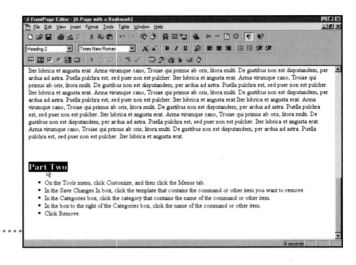

1 Begin by opening two pages in FrontPage Editor, just as you did in Task 30. Use the **Window** menu to display the destination page in the FrontPage Editor workspace. Scroll through the page until you find the text you want for the bookmark, then select that text.

2 Open the **Edit** menu and click **Bookmark**.

3 In the Bookmark dialog box, you can accept the supplied name for the bookmark (it's the text you selected) or you can type a new bookmark name in the Bookmark Name text box. When you're satisfied with the name, click **OK**.

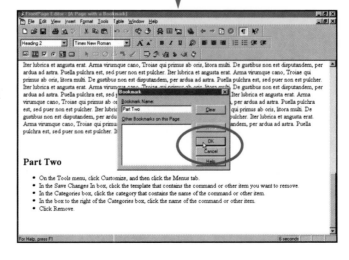

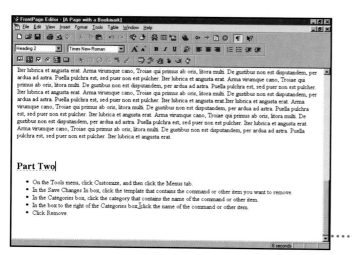

4 The dialog box closes. Click once anywhere to remove the black highlighting around the bookmark text. You'll see the text now has a blue dotted underline. This is the standard way of identifying a bookmark. (The dotted line doesn't show up in a browser.) Now save the page by opening the **File** menu and clicking the **Save** option.

5 Now open the **Window** menu and click the name of the page with the link to the bookmark. When the page appears in the workspace, select the text that is to be the link. Then open the **Edit** menu and click **Hyperlink** to open the Create Hyperlink dialog box. If the Open Pages sheet isn't on top, click the **Open Pages** tab to make it so.

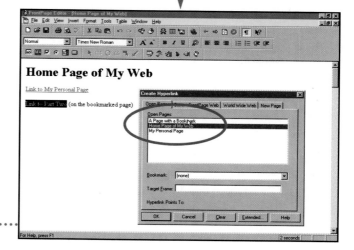

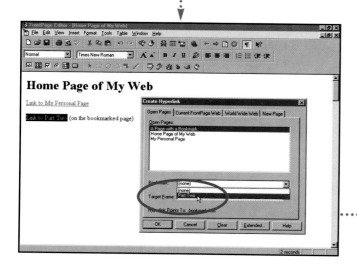

6 In the Open Pages list box, click the name of the page that has the bookmark. Then, click the arrow button at the right of the Bookmark box. From the drop-down list, click the name of the bookmark you made on the destination page.

7 Click **OK** to close the dialog box. Click once anywhere to remove the highlight from the linked text, and you'll see that the text is now blue and underlined—it's a hyperlink to the bookmark on the destination page.

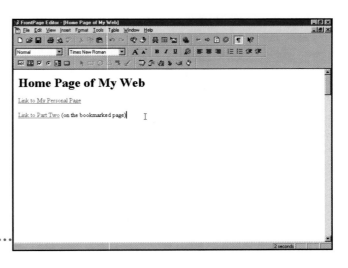

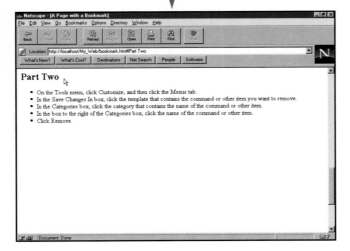

8 Open the **File** menu and click the **Preview in Browser** option. Choose a browser, and click **Preview**. The destination page should appear with the bookmarked text showing in the browser window. ■

Puzzled?

If the bookmark link took you to the top of the destination page and not to the bookmarked section, it's likely you didn't save the bookmarked page. Close the browser, save the bookmarked page, and try Step 8 again.

TASK **33**

Linking to a Closed Page

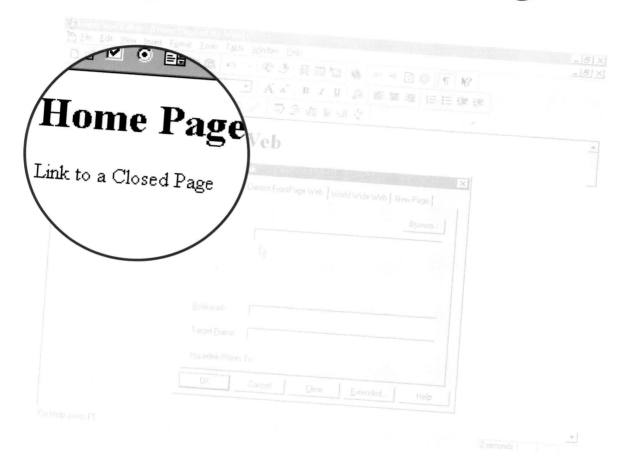

"Why would I do this?"

This is really more of a shortcut than a feature.
It simply lets you make a link to an existing
page within the opened Web site, even if that
page isn't actually loaded into FrontPage Editor.
It saves you the bother of opening the destination page.

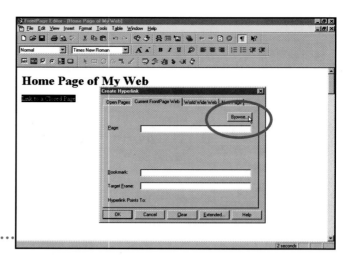

1 Select the text for the link. Then open the **Edit** menu and click the **Hyperlink** option. When the Create Hyperlink dialog box appears, click the **Current FrontPage Web** tab to put the Current FrontPage Web sheet on top.

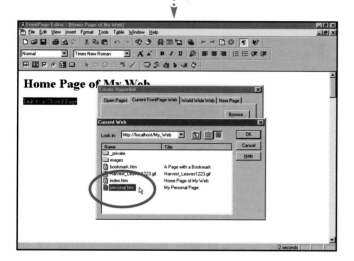

2 Click the **Browse** button to open the Current Web dialog box. In the large list box, find the Name of the destination page and click it. Then click **OK** to close the Current Web dialog box. Click **OK** again to close the Create Hyperlink dialog box, and the link is set up. ■

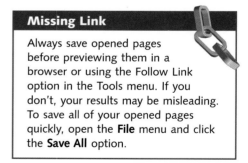

Missing Link

Always save opened pages before previewing them in a browser or using the Follow Link option in the Tools menu. If you don't, your results may be misleading. To save all of your opened pages quickly, open the **File** menu and click the **Save All** option.

Linking to a New Page

"Why would I do this?"

Again, this is more of a time-saver than a major tool. It allows you to create a Web page and set up a link to it all in one go. It's handy if you're in a hurry to meet a deadline!

1 Select the text for the link. Then open the **Edit** menu and click the **Hyperlink** option. When the Create Hyperlink dialog box appears, click the **New Page** tab to put the New Page sheet on top.

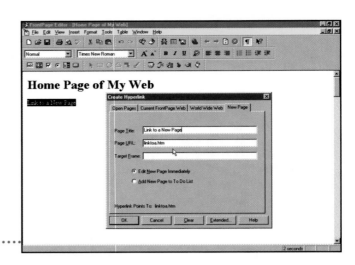

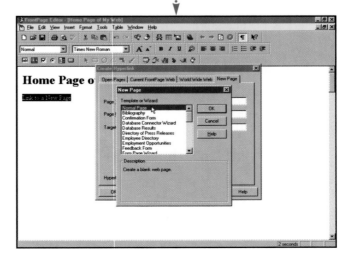

2 The Page Title text box repeats the text you've selected for the link. If you don't want that text to be the Page Title, type a new title into the Page Title text box. Now look at the Page URL text box. The entry here is the page file name in your currently opened Web. (FrontPage Editor bases it on the Page Title.) If you want a different file name, type that into the Page URL text box. Then mark the **Edit New Page Immediately** radio button, and click **OK**.

3 The New Page dialog box appears. Select the type of page you want, and click **OK**. The link to the new page is created, and the new page appears in the FrontPage Editor workspace, ready for editing. ■

Linking to a World Wide Web

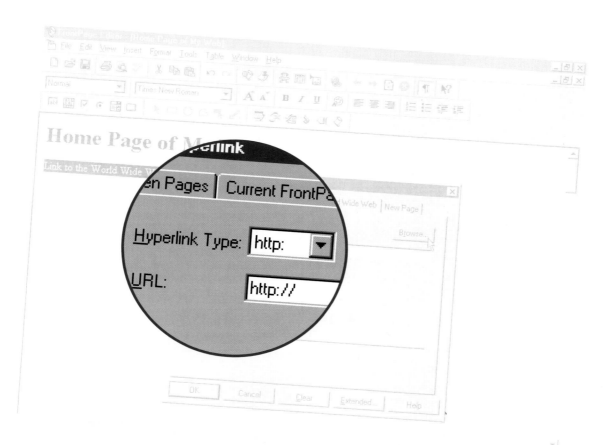

"Why would I do this?"

It's now that you'll get a real sense of the power of hyperlinks. Local hyperlinks are useful things, but connecting your pages to the World Wide Web puts vast resources at your disposal and at the disposal of your visitors. Give them useful links to follow, and they'll return to your page again and again.

1 First make sure your PC is connected to the Internet. Then start FrontPage, and in FrontPage Editor open the page where you want the link. Create and/or select the text for the link, then open the **Edit** menu and click **Hyperlink**. In the Create Hyperlink dialog box, click the **World Wide Web** tab to put the World Wide Web sheet on top.

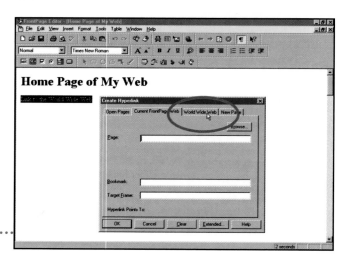

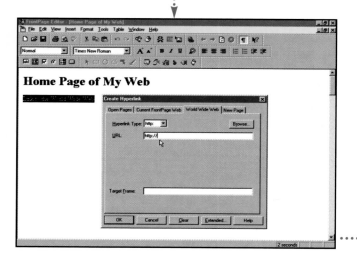

2 Click in the text box labeled URL so that the blinking insertion point is right after the **http//**. Then click **Browse**.

3 FrontPage Editor opens an Internet Explorer browser window with the message: "Find the page you want to link to, then switch back to FrontPage." Use the browser to find and display the destination page of the link.

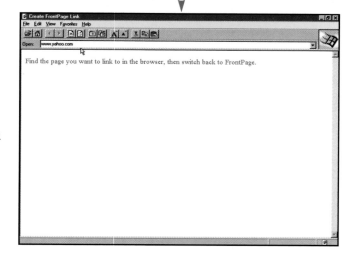

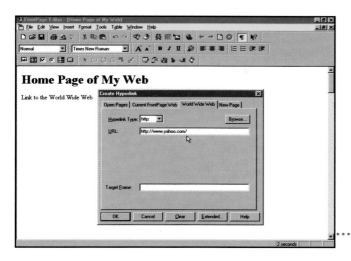

4 When the desired page appears in the browser window, don't close the browser. Instead, use the Windows 95 Taskbar to switch back to FrontPage Editor. Now, you'll see the page's URL (its World Wide Web address) in the URL text box. Click **OK**. The dialog box closes, and you can see on your own page that the link has been created (it's in blue text with underlining).

5 Use the Windows 95 taskbar to switch back to the browser window. In the browser, open the **File** menu and click **Exit** to close the browser. If you want to use the File menu's Preview in Browser option to test the link, you have to leave your PC connected to the Internet. After you've finished all your testing, you can close down your Internet connection. ■

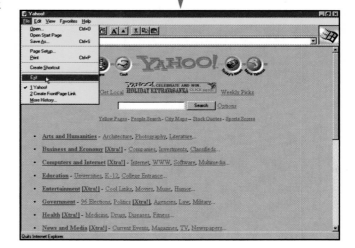

Missing Link

If you know the URL of the destination page, you can type it into the URL text box right after the **http://** and click **OK**. With this technique, you don't need to connect your PC to the Internet, because you don't need to use Browse. But, be sure you type the destination page's URL correctly!

Changing Links

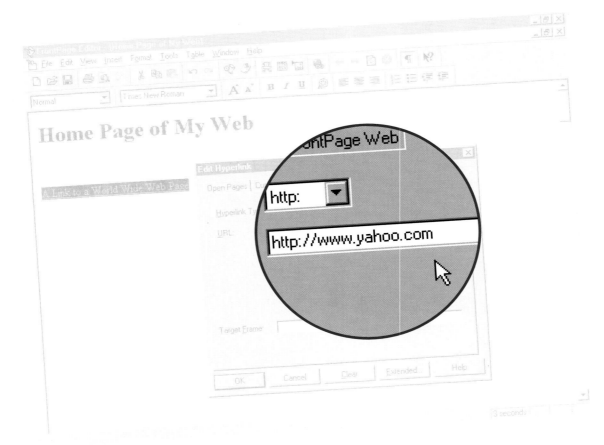

"Why would I do this?"

You need to change a link ("edit a link") if the
address of its destination page changes. If you
don't, you and your Web site's visitors will get
an error message when the link is clicked. Since
no one likes error messages, it's a good idea to
check your links regularly and keep them up to
date. Sometimes, of course, you've simply inserted a typographical error into the address you
assigned to the link.

112

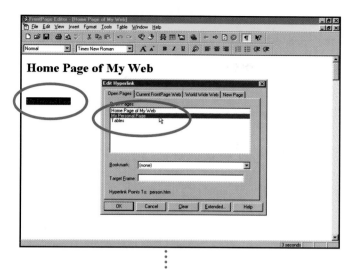

1 In FrontPage Editor, open the page with the incorrect link. Click the link. Then open the **Edit** menu and click **Hyperlink**. The Edit Hyperlink dialog box appears. If the link is a link to a page currently opened in FrontPage Editor, the Open Page sheet will be on top. Then, in the Open Pages list box, click the page that the link is supposed to point to. Then click **OK**.

2 If the link is to an unopened page, the top sheet is "Current FrontPage Web." You can type the correct file name of the page into the Page text box. Alternatively, you can click **Browse** and select the proper destination page from the Current Web dialog box, as you did in Task 33. (Again, in the example, the incorrect destination is "Tables," and is being changed to "My Personal Page.") When you're done, click **OK** to close the Current Web dialog box, and **OK** again to close the Edit Hyperlink dialog box.

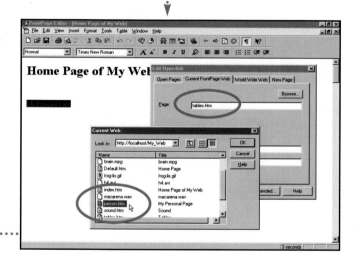

3 If the link is to a page on the World Wide Web, the World Wide Web sheet will be on top. To change the link, you can click **Browse** and use the method from Task 35. You can also just retype the link into the URL text box, but if you do this, be sure you don't delete the **http://** at the beginning of the link—change only the text after the **http://**. Otherwise, the link won't work at all.

4 You can change the "protocol" of the link. The **http://** "protocol" links only to Web pages. But, suppose you want to link to an FTP site or a Gopher site? To do this, click the arrow button at the right end of the Hyperlink Type drop-down list box. Click the link you want. Then click Browse.

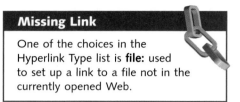

Missing Link

One of the choices in the Hyperlink Type list is **file:** used to set up a link to a file not in the currently opened Web.

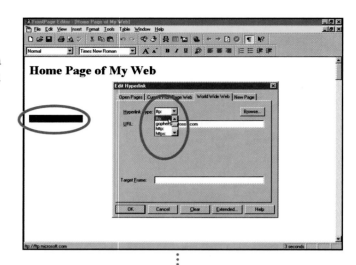

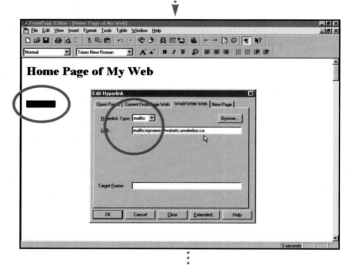

5 You may want your e-mail address on your site, so people can communicate with you. For this, use the mailto type of link. You just click **mailto:** in the Hyperlink Type drop-down list box, then type your e-mail address into the URL text box, right after the **mailto:** entry. Click **OK** to set up the link. Now, when someone clicks the link, it automatically starts the e-mail program he uses on his machine, and he can write to you.

6 You might want to direct someone to a newsgroup from your site. To do this, select **news:** in the Hyperlink Type drop-down list box, then type the newsgroup name into the URL text box right after the **news:** entry. Click **OK** to set up the link. Now, when someone clicks the link, the news reader on his machine will automatically start and connect to the newsgroup. ■

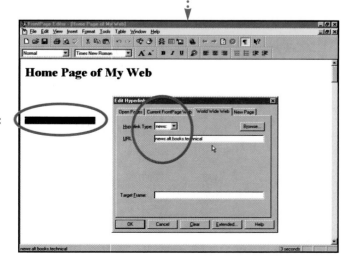

Removing a Link

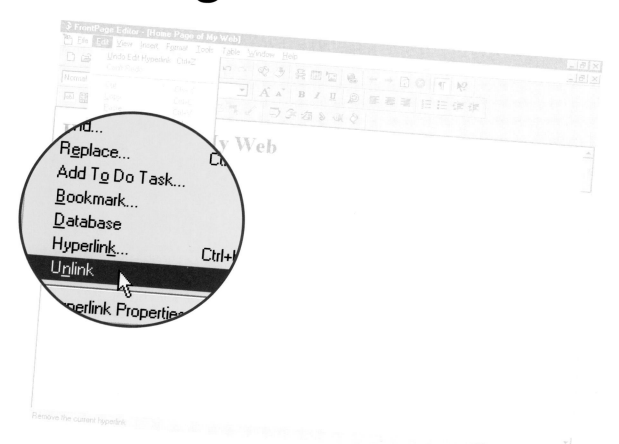

"Why would I do this?"

You may have created a link to a page of your own and some time later decided to delete that page. Or you may have linked to a page that has vanished from another World Wide Web site. (Whole sites sometimes vanish, too!) If this happens, it's professional to remove the link as soon as possible. Visitors don't like sites with a lot of defective links, or "dead links" as they're called.

1 To remove a link, click it. Then open the **Edit** menu and click the **Unlink** option. This removes the linking itself, though not the text. Remove the text, if you need to, by selecting it and pressing the **Delete** key.

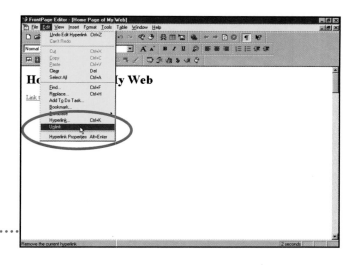

2 The second way to remove a link is to click it once, then open the **Edit** menu, then click **Hyperlink**. When the Edit Hyperlink dialog box appears, click **Clear** and then click **OK**. ■

Missing Link

Sometimes, you want to delete not only a link but also the text you used for it. To do this, select all of the link text and press the **Delete** key. Just make sure you get all the text—even an undeleted space will keep the link active. The two preceding methods are more trustworthy than this one.

PART IV

Working with Images, Color, and Multimedia

PART IV TELLS YOU HOW TO PUT IMAGES onto your page, how to lay out text and graphics together, and how to use graphics as links. You also learn the basics of Image Composer, and how to use sound and video in your Web pages.

Traditional print resources usually give the reader long blocks of unbroken text to read. This works fine on the printed page, but dense text doesn't look all that good on computer monitors. Even the best computer displays can't equal the clarity of print on paper, and studies have shown that people read more slowly from a screen than they do from a page in a book. As a result, most people dislike slogging through screens crammed with words. So, if that's all your Web site offers them, they'll likely go elsewhere—even if both the information and writing style are good.

When a page appears in a browser, what attracts the eye first are its images. Well chosen, interesting ones entice a visitor into looking deeper into the page content; if the content is also good, she's likely to think well of your Web site and bookmark it for future visits. So, images are a resource no Web page author should willingly do without.

Images, also referred to as graphics, are a little trickier to use than text. Images have to be sent from your page to the viewer's browser before he can see them; this is called "downloading a graphic." Graphics are stored in graphics files, and a large color image can require a big file. Big files take longer to download than small files, and many people won't wait a long time to see a picture. A good rule of thumb is to keep your graphics files to 20K or less; some authorities even suggest that all the images on a page should total no more than this.

The two most common graphic-file formats for Web pages are GIF (Graphics Interchange Format), and JPEG (Joint Photographic Experts Group). All graphics-capable browsers display these two formats without fuss. Both formats are "compressed"; that is, the file is squeezed down in size when it's sent to a browser, and the browser "decompresses" or expands it so it displays correctly. But which format should you use in your pages?

Each has advantages. Browsers decompress GIFs quickly, so GIF images show up fairly briskly on your visitor's screen. It's the preferred format for line art; that is, art without the continuous shading of photographs. GIF image files do tend to be larger than equivalent JPEG ones, so what you gain in fast GIF decompression you lose (somewhat) in having to store bigger files on your site. On the other hand, JPEG files, while they're smaller to begin with, decompress more slowly than GIF files. Their advantage over GIFs is they're better at reproducing continuous-tone images on the screen. Generally speaking, use GIFs for line art and flat-color images, and JPEG for continuous-tone images. A GIF image can have up to 256 colors; a JPEG can have up to 16.7 million.

Some images, especially icons and buttons, are available on the Internet for free use. However, to customize your Web site, you'll likely want graphics of your own. You can produce original artwork with graphics packages, such as the Image Composer included with FrontPage 97. Or you can use paint or photography to make physical images, and then use a scanner to transform them into JPEG or GIF files. Then you can import the images into your Web, and insert them into your pages.

TASK

38

Importing an Image into Your Web

"Why would I do this?"

To put an image (also called a "graphic") on your Web page, you naturally have to have a file that contains the image. Web images are usually saved in GIF or JPEG graphics file formats; the file extensions are .gif and .jpg.

It's convenient to have all the images for a Web stored in that Web, and importing image files is a handy way to achieve this. This task shows you how to import "GIFs" or "JPEGs" (as they're called) into a FrontPage Web from any folder on your PC's hard drive, floppy drive, or CD-ROM drive.

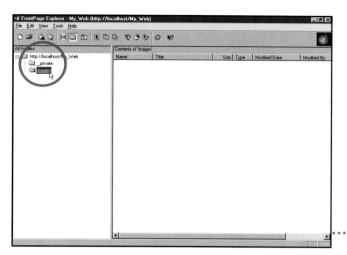

1 Start FrontPage and open a Web in FrontPage Explorer. Open the **View** menu and click **Folder** View. In the left pane, click the **images** folder. This folder is where we'll store the images for your Web. With a newly created Web, the right pane of Folder View will be empty.

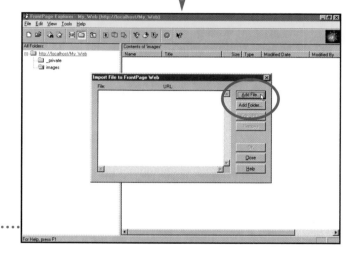

2 Open the **File** menu and click **Import** to open the Import File to FrontPage Web dialog box. In the dialog box, click **Add File**.

3 The Add File to Import List dialog box opens. Except for the dialog title, this is a normal Windows 95 file dialog.

4 Use the Look In drop-down list and then the dialog list box to locate the folder on your hard disk, floppy drive, or CD-ROM, where the graphics files are stored. (Your folders and file names will be different from those shown in the pictures.) Then click **Open**.

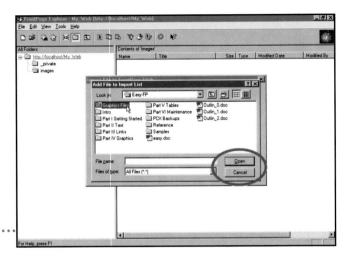

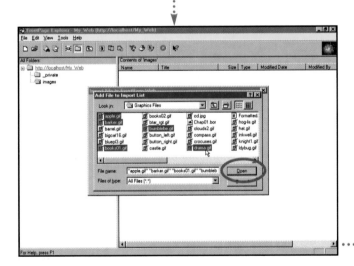

5 In the list box of the Add File to Import List dialog, use the usual Windows 95 techniques to select the GIF or JPEG file or files you want to import. When you've selected them, click **Open** again.

6 The Import File to FrontPage Web dialog box reappears, with the names of the selected files in the list box.

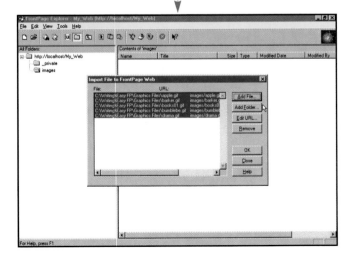

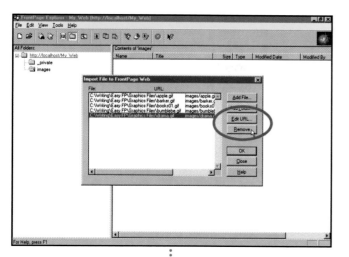

7 To remove a file, click its name and then click **Remove**. To add another file, click **Add File** and repeat Steps 3 through 5. When the import list is correct, click **OK**. The list of file names shortens as the files are imported, and when they're all gone the dialog box disappears.

Puzzled?

The Close button closes the dialog box without starting the import. When you open the **File** menu again and click **Import**, the import list is still there. It's just a convenience.

8 Make sure the **images** folder is selected, and in the right pane of FrontPage Explorer's Folder View, you'll see the names of the imported files. Now they're easily available for use in FrontPage Editor. ■

Missing Link

You can, in fact, store the images in the main Web folder, where the pages are listed, but it's better organization to put them into the images folder. You can also import an entire folder and its contents by clicking **Add Folder** in the Import File to FrontPage Web dialog box.

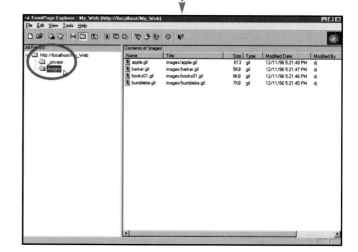

TASK

39

Putting an Image onto a Page

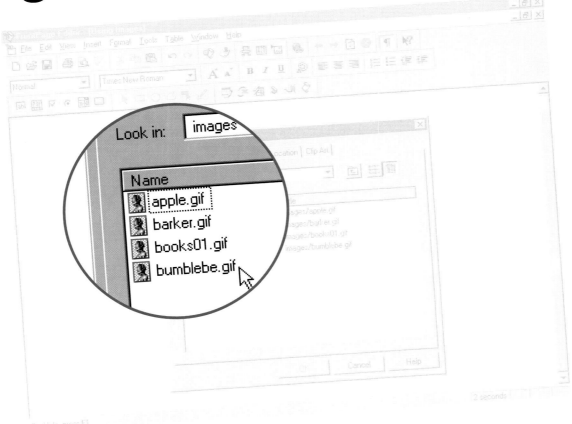

"Why would I do this?"

Images add visual interest to your pages, provide information, amplify the meaning of text, break text into manageable chunks, and give your site character. They are now an integral part of almost all World Wide Web sites, and human nature being what it is, your visitors these days will expect you to give them some color and style. If your site is nothing but black text on a gray or white background, you won't hold anyone's interest for long.

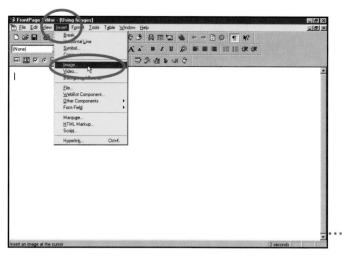

1 Decide where you want to place the top-left corner of the image, and click once at that position to place the insertion point there. Then open the **Insert** menu and click **Image**.

2 In the Image dialog box, if the Current FrontPage Web sheet isn't on top, click the **Current FrontPage Web** tab to bring it to the top. In the list box, double-click the icon of the **images** folder (you have to double-click it, because the OK button is disabled at this point).

3 A list of the images in the images folder appears. Click the name of the image you want to place on the page. Then click **OK**.

125

4 The dialog box closes, and the image appears on the page.

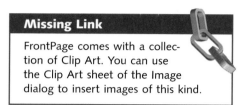

Missing Link

FrontPage comes with a collection of Clip Art. You can use the Clip Art sheet of the Image dialog to insert images of this kind.

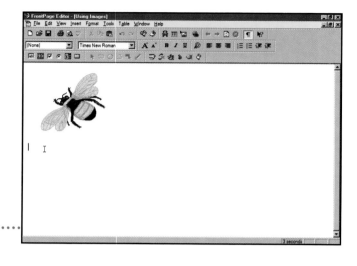

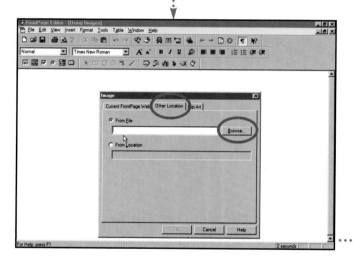

5 If you haven't imported the image to your Web, you can do so from the Image dialog box. To do this, open the Image dialog box, and click the **Other Location** tab. Then click **Browse**.

6 The next dialog box is a standard Windows 95 file location dialog box. Use the Look In drop-down box and the list box to find the drive and folder where the image is stored. Your folder and file names will be different from those shown.

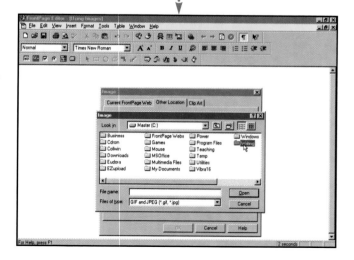

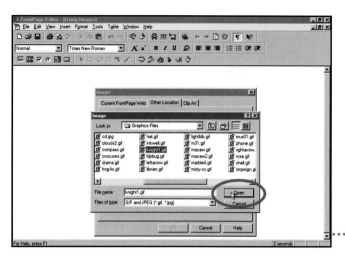

7 When you locate the name of the image, click it. Then click **Open**.

8 When the image appears on the page, open the **File** menu and click the **Save** option. When the Save Image to FrontPage Web dialog box appears, click **Yes**. Note that this saves the image to the folder that contains the Web pages themselves.

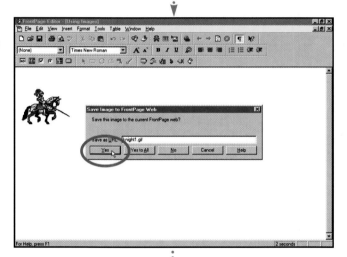

Missing Link

To force the Save Image to FrontPage Web dialog box to put the image in the images folder, insert the text **images/** ahead of the file name in the Save As URL text box. Based on the example shown, that box would then read **images/ knight1.gif** and the image would end up in the images folder when you click **Yes**.

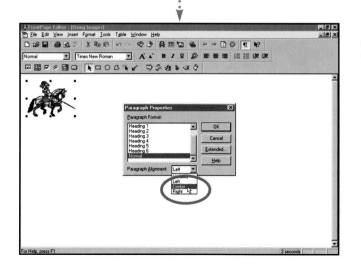

9 To move an image from the left margin, click the image once to select it. (You know it's selected when small black squares appear around the image.) Then open the **Format** menu and click **Paragraph**. Click the arrow button at the right of the Paragraph alignment box, and when the drop-down list appears click either **Center** or **Right**. Then click **OK**, and the image will be centered or placed at the right margin, respectively. ∎

127

Deleting an Image

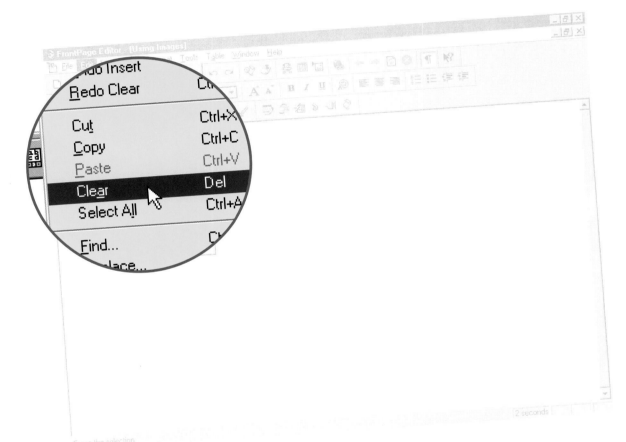

"Why would I do this?"

Everybody makes mistakes, even professional designers, and you'll discover from time to time that a particular graphic just doesn't work out the way you thought it would. Fortunately, deleting an image is a lot simpler than getting it onto the page!

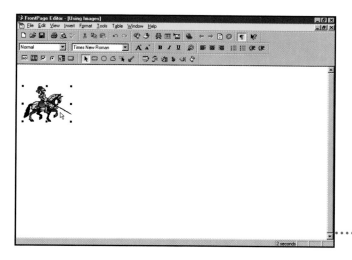

1 First, select the graphic. This simply means click it somewhere. You know a graphic is selected when it's surrounded by little black squares.

Puzzled?

To deselect a graphic, click anywhere outside the boundary outlined by the little black squares.

2 Open the **Edit** menu and choose the **Clear** option. The graphic disappears.

Missing Link

If you prefer a keyboard technique, just select the graphic and press the **Delete** key.

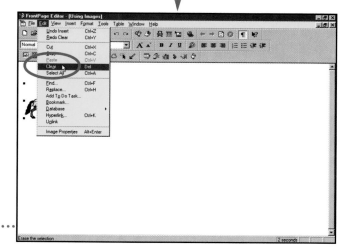

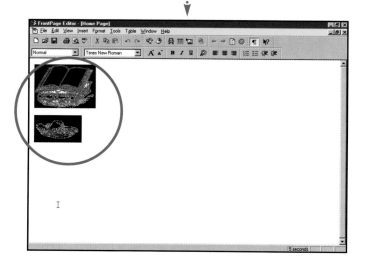

3 To delete multiple images, first drag across them to select them. They'll appear in reverse video when selected. Then open the **Edit** menu and click the **Clear** option (or just press the **Delete** key). ■

TASK **41**

Positioning Text Around an Image

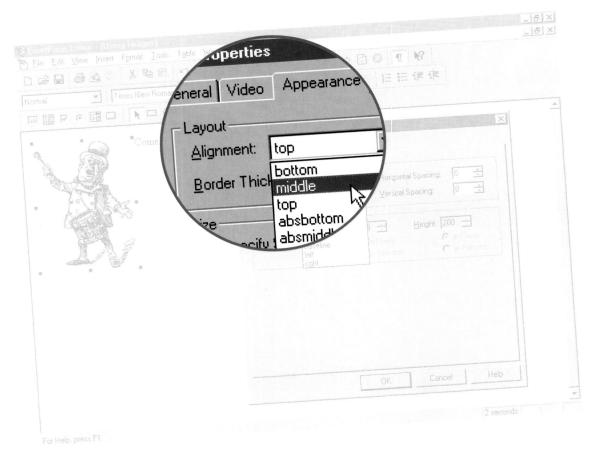

"Why would I do this?"

When you finish inserting an image, the blinking insertion point appears immediately to its right. If you now type a line of text, the bottom of the text lines up with

the bottom of the image. Sometimes, though, you'd prefer it if the text line were positioned halfway up the side of the image, or at its top. This task shows you how to get these effects.

130

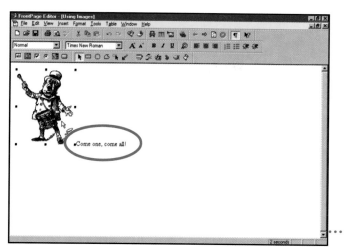

1 The text here is lined up with the bottom of the image. To put it halfway up the side of the image, first select the image by clicking it. You know the image is selected when small black squares appear around it.

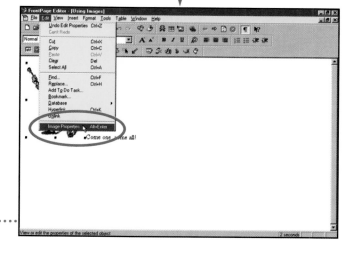

2 Open the **Edit** menu and click the **Image Properties** option.

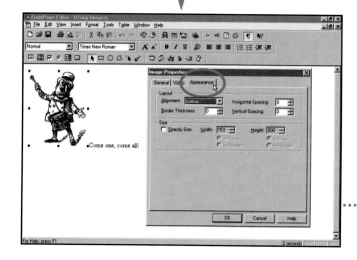

3 In the ImageProperties dialog box, click the **Appearance** tab to bring the Appearance sheet to the top.

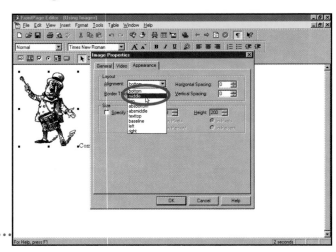

4 In the Layout section of this sheet, click the arrow button at the right of the Alignment box. In the drop-down list, click **Middle**.

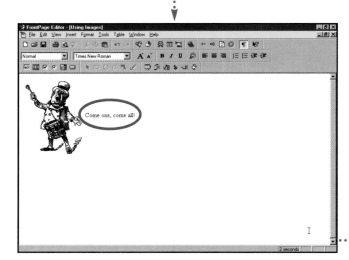

5 Click **OK**. Now, the text is positioned halfway up the side of the image. Click anywhere outside the image to deselect it.

6 To line up the text with the top edge of the image, repeat Steps 1 through 4. In Step 4, instead of clicking Middle in the Alignment drop-down list, click **Top**. Then click **OK**. ■

Puzzled?

With this method you're restricted to placing a single line of text in the Middle or Top positions. Task 43 shows you how to "wrap" text so that it flows completely around the image.

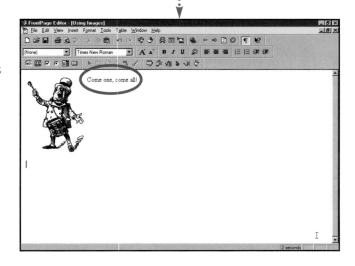

Making an Image "Float"

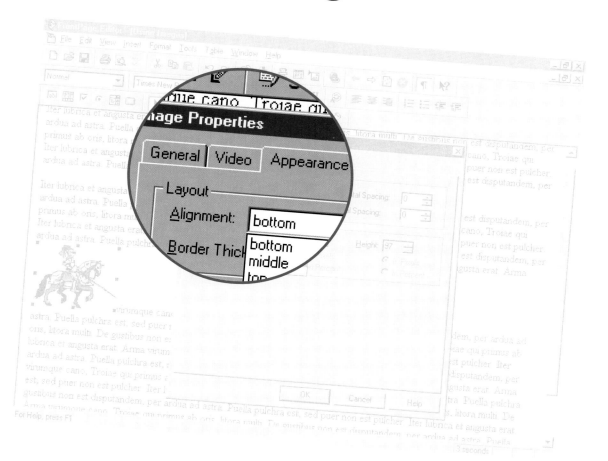

"Why would I do this?"

When you're laying out the text and graphics on a page, you'll often find that things look better if the text flows all around the image. To get this effect you make an image "float" at the left or right edge of a page.

Task 42: Making an Image "Float"

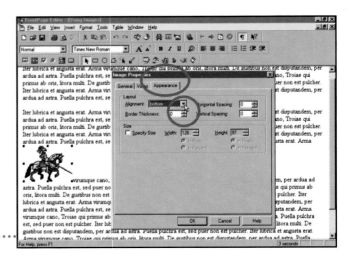

1 First, click once on the image to select it. Then open the **Edit** menu and click **Image Properties**. When the Image Properties dialog box appears, click the **Appearance** tab to put the Appearance sheet on top.

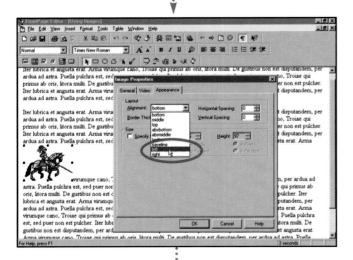

2 In the Layout section, click the arrow button at the right of the Alignment box. When the drop-down list appears, click **Left** or **Right**, depending on which side of the page you want the image.

Missing Link

You can adjust the spacing between the image and text by changing the numbers in the Horizontal Spacing and Vertical Spacing boxes of the Appearance sheet.

3 Click **OK**. The text wraps around the image. Click anywhere outside the image to deselect it. ■

Puzzled?

With a floating image, you'll see a small, black rectangle somewhere near it. This isn't a leftover selection mark—it's associated with the image itself. Ignore it; it doesn't show up in a browser. (If you accidentally delete it, the image will be deleted, too!)

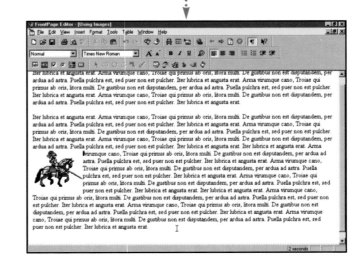

Providing Alternative Text

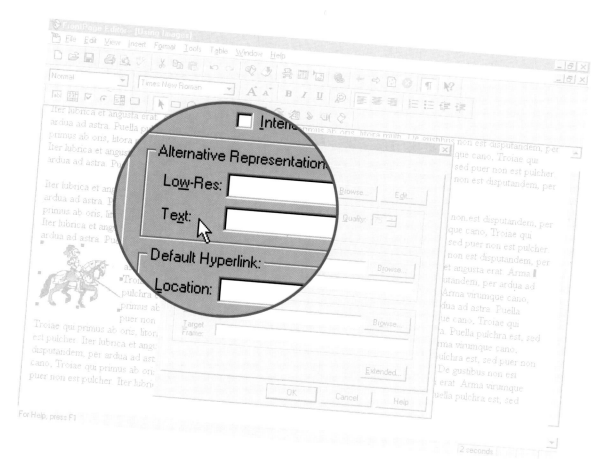

"Why would I do this?"

Many people, to make pages appear faster in their browsers, operate the browser with the images option turned off. This means they don't see the image when the page loads, only image placeholders. (Recent browsers load images after text, so the placeholders appear for awhile

even if images are turned on in the browser.) These placeholders should have a text label to suggest to the viewer what the image actually is. Usually, this label is called "alternative text."

Task 43: Providing Alternative Text

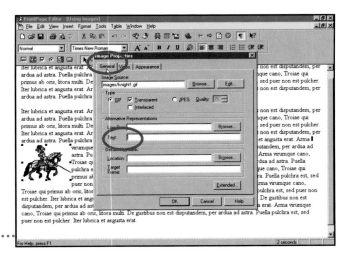

1 Select the image, then open the **Edit** menu and click the **Image Properties** option. When the Image Properties dialog box appears, click the **General** tab if the General sheet isn't already on top.

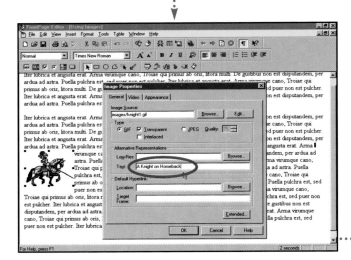

2 In the Alternative Representations section, click in the Text text box to place the insertion point there, and type a very brief label for the image.

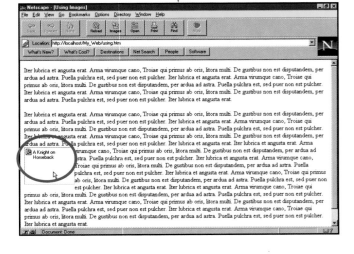

3 When a browser with images turned off displays this page, the viewer will see the descriptive label of the image. ■

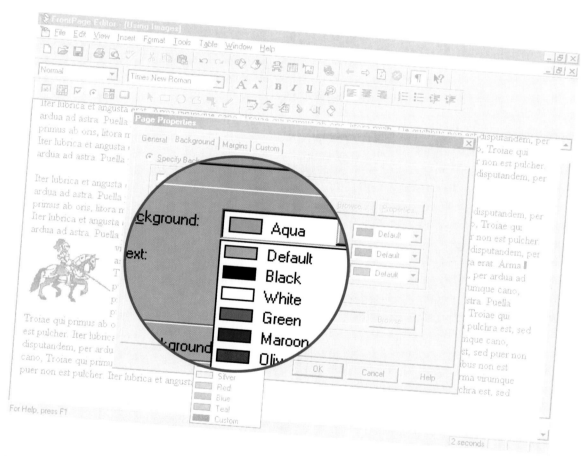

Changing the Page Color

"Why would I do this?"

Both content and presentation are important in a Web page, and one element of the presentation is the page's color scheme. The basic Web page scheme, black text on gray, is drab if not downright ugly. You can change both background and text colors easily with FrontPage, but don't go overboard. An exotic color scheme may be striking on first appearance, but if it gives your visitor a headache, he'll go elsewhere.

Task 44: Changing the Page Color

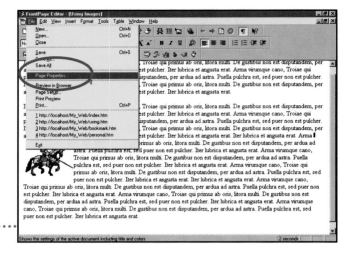

1 With the page open in FrontPage Editor, open the **File** menu and click the **Page Properties** option.

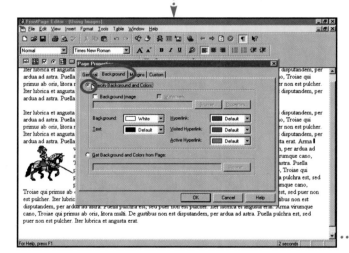

2 When the Page Properties dialog box appears, click the **Background** tab to put the Background sheet on top. If the Specify Background and Colors radio button isn't already marked, click it to mark it.

3 To change the page background color, click the button at the right of the Background drop-down list box. A drop-down list of available colors appears. Click the one you want to select it.

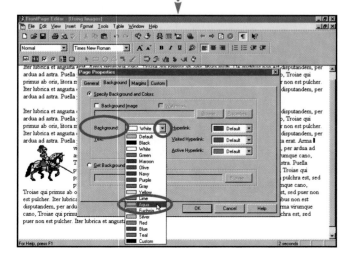

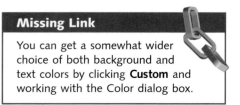

Missing Link

You can get a somewhat wider choice of both background and text colors by clicking **Custom** and working with the Color dialog box.

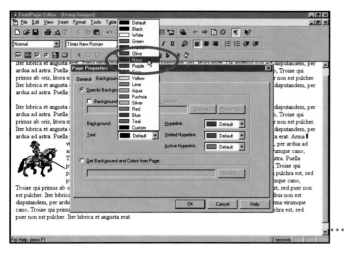

4 To change the text color, click the button at the right of the Text drop-down list box. A drop-down list of available colors appears. Click the one you want to select it.

5 Click **OK**. The dialog box closes and the new color scheme appears in all its glory. ■

Missing Link

Don't bother using color depths over 8-bit (256 colors). Most people's systems are set up for 256 colors at most, and using subtle hues beyond these is a waste of your time.

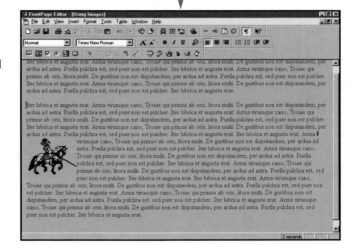

TASK 45

Creating a Hyperlink from an Image

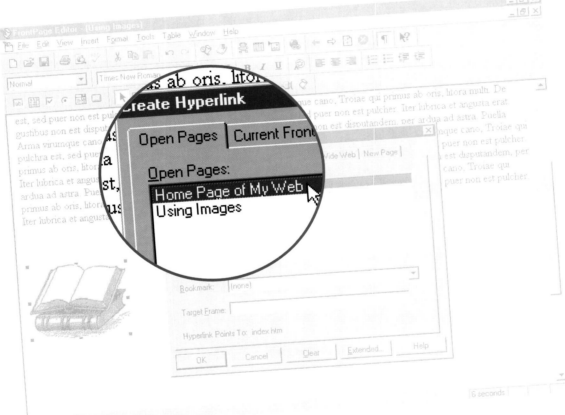

"Why would I do this?"

Image-based links are very common on Web pages. They are more interesting to the eye than text links, though you should ensure their appearance makes it clear that such an image is also a link. Using them in combination with text links add variety and visual appeal to your pages.

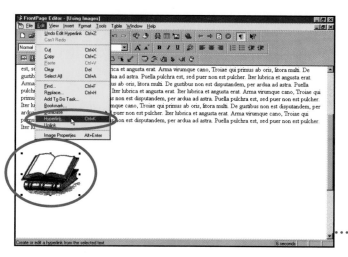

1 Select the image you want to use for the link by clicking it. Then, open the **Edit** menu and click the **Hyperlink** option.

2 The Create Hyperlink dialog box appears. This is identical to the dialog box used to create text hyperlinks. Use the methods you learned in Tasks 31, 34, 35, 36, and 37 to set up the link. ■

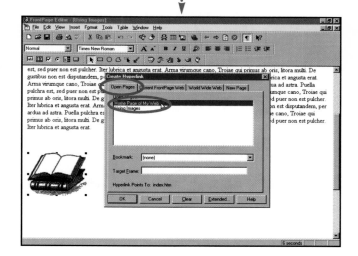

Puzzled?

You change an image-based link the same way you change a text link. Click the image to select it, then use the editing techniques you learned in Task 38.

Missing Link

If you want an image-based link to have an accompanying text link that points to the same location, you can set up both the image-based link and the text link at the same time. Drag over the image and the text to select them both, then use the methods you learned in Tasks 31, 34, 35, 36, and 37 to set up the link.

Creating Image Maps

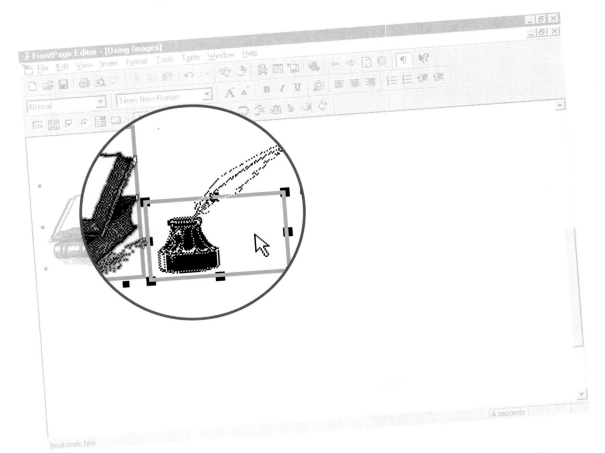

"Why would I do this?"

Image maps give you another way of designing links into your pages. An image map is a graphic that has "hotspots" in it. These hotspots are actually links; when a viewer clicks a hotspot, she's automatically sent to another location in your Web, or in the World Wide Web or the Internet. To put it another way, image maps are graphics with links stuffed into them.

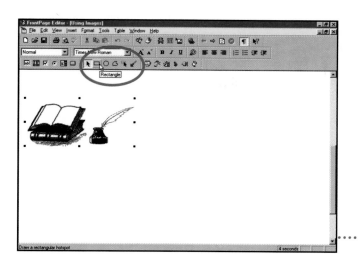

1 Click the graphic you're going to use as the image map. With the graphic selected, look at the Image Toolbar. On your screen, it may not be where it's shown in the illustration. (If it's not visible at all, open the **View** menu and click the **Image Toolbar** option.)

2 Slide the mouse onto the small hollow rectangle on the Image Toolbar, then click the rectangle once. This selects the drawing tool that makes a rectangular hotspot. Slide the mouse onto the image, and a little pencil appears.

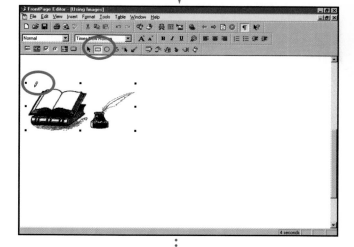

Missing Link

You can also select a circle/ellipse drawing tool or a polygon tool from the Image Toolbar.

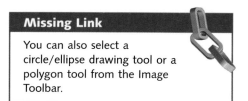

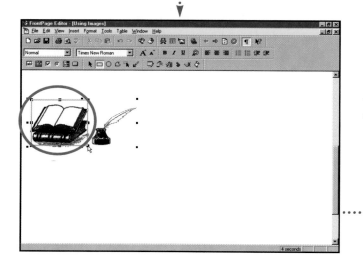

3 Hold the left mouse button down, and drag the pencil. A rectangular outline appears as you drag. Make it the size you want, then release the left mouse button.

143

4 As soon as you release the mouse button, the Create Hyperlink dialog box appears. Set up the link for the hotspot, using the techniques you learned in Tasks 31, 34, 35, 36, or 37. Then click **OK** to leave the Create Hyperlink dialog box. Repeat Steps 2 through 4 to create more hotspots and links until you're finished. Then click anywhere outside the graphic to make the hotspot outlines disappear.

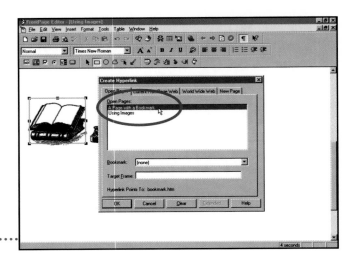

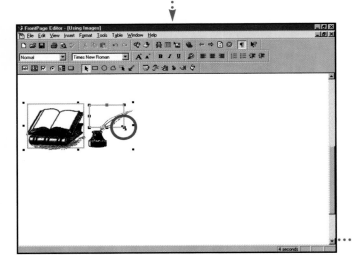

5 To adjust the size of a hotspot, click the image, then click the hotspot to be sized. Slide the mouse onto one of the little black squares that bound the hotspot. This square is a sizing handle. When you see a double-headed arrow, hold down the left mouse button and drag the handle to resize the hotspot.

6 To adjust a hotspot's position on the graphic, slide the mouse inside the hotspot boundaries, hold down the left mouse button, and drag. When the hotspot is positioned correctly, release the mouse button. ∎

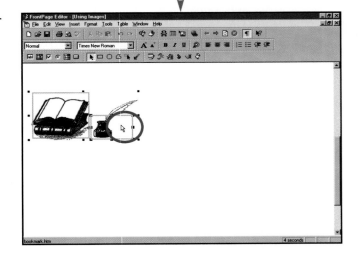

Puzzled?

To delete a hotspot and its link, click inside the hotspot once and press the **Delete** key. To edit a hotspot's link, open the **Edit** menu and click **Hyperlink**. Then use the techniques you learned in Task 38.

Creating a Graphic with Image Composer

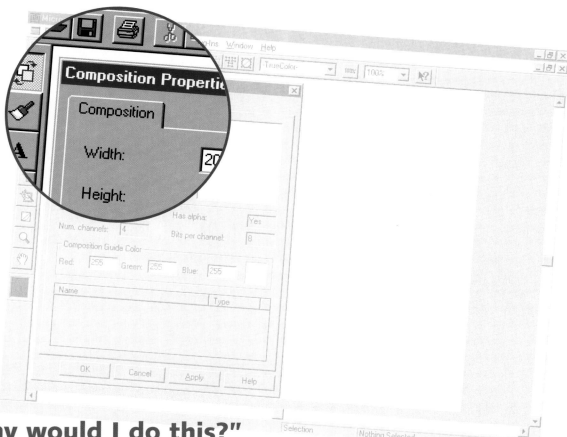

"Why would I do this?"

The best Web sites have an individual character, often provided largely by the graphics that appear on the site's pages. If you want this sense of individuality for your own Web, then off-the-shelf pictures (the kind you can download from the Internet) probably won't do very well. Image Composer will help you create some original-looking images, even if you aren't a graphics designer. Before we begin this task, put your Microsoft FrontPage 97 installation CD in your CD-ROM drive—the CD has Image Composer's image files on it. If the FrontPage 97 install window appears after you insert the CD, just close the window—you don't need it.

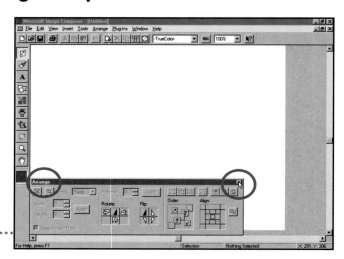

1 With a page open in FrontPage Editor, open the **Tools** menu and click **Show Image Editor**. When the Image Composer screen appears, find the Arrange dialog box and close it; we don't need it for this example.

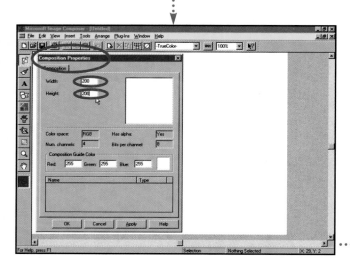

2 Image Composer starts off with a sheet of "paper" (the white area in the workspace) that is rather large for a Web page graphic, so we'll reduce its size. Open the **File** menu and click **Composition Properties**. In the Composition Properties dialog box, type **200** into the Width box and **200** into the Height box. Then click **OK**. The size of our "paper" is now about right.

3 Open the **Insert** menu and click **From File**. A standard Windows 95 file dialog box opens, with the dialog title Insert From File. Use this dialog to go to your CD-ROM drive. Your folder and drive names may be different from those shown.

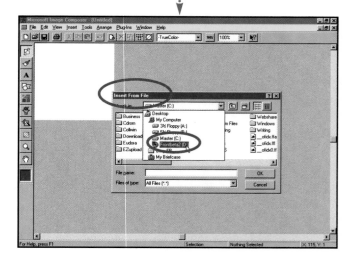

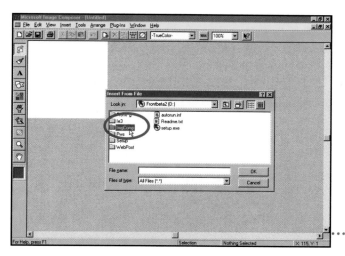

4 When the folders on your FrontPage 97 CD appear in the Insert From File dialog list box, double-click **ImgComp**.

5 A new set of folders appears in the list box. Double-click **Mmfiles**.

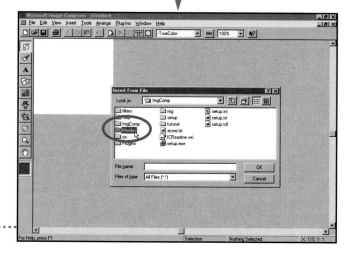

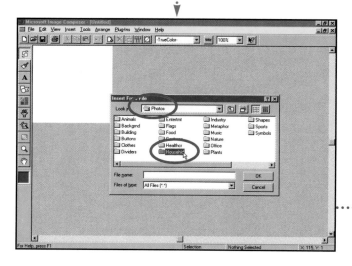

6 A new set of folders appears in the list box. Double-click **Photos**. This Photos folder has a lot of other folders in it, which contain images. To follow the example, double-click the **Househld** folder that is in the Photos folder.

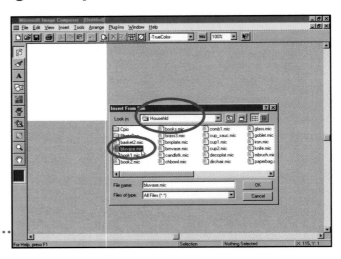

7 In the list box, click **bluvase.mic**. Then click **OK**.

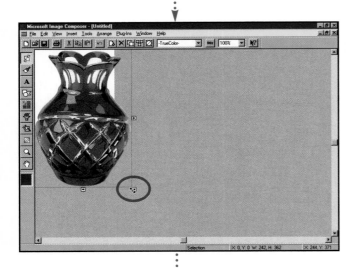

8 A blue vase appears, too big for our sheet of paper. Slide the mouse to the small arrow (a sizing handle) at the lower-right corner of the graphic, so the mouse cursor becomes a double-headed arrow. Then hold the Shift key down, hold the left mouse button down, and drag the corner of the graphic until it's small enough to fit on the paper. Then release the mouse button, and next the Shift key (using the Shift key preserves the proportions of the image).

9 To adjust the image's positioning on the paper, slide the mouse inside the image boundaries. A four-headed arrow appears. Hold down the left mouse button, drag the image to its new position, and release the mouse button.

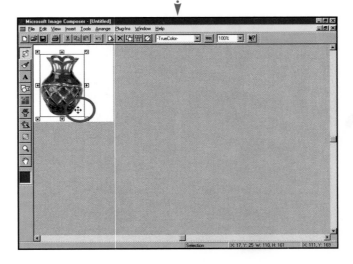

Missing Link

Be careful that none of the image is off the "paper." Anything not on the paper will be cut off when the image is saved.

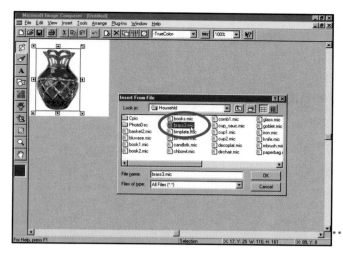

10 Let's add another image to the sheet of paper. Open the **Insert** menu, and click **From File**. The list box will be the same as in Step 7. Click **brass3mic**, then click **OK**.

11 The brass bucket appears at the top left of the paper. This is small, so you don't need to resize it. Drag it to a suitable place on the paper.

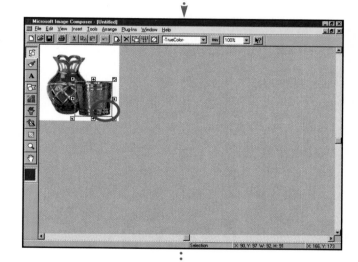

Missing Link

If you need the highest possible image clarity, use the JPEG format. This makes the file larger, though, so if you want a small file that will appear quickly in a browser, use the GIF format instead.

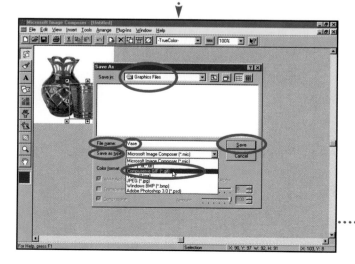

12 Open the **File** menu and click **Save As**. In the Save As dialog box, use the Save In box to choose a folder where the image will be saved. In the File Name box, type a name for the image. Then, since Web graphics are usually in GIF or JPEG format, click the arrow button at the right of the Save as Type box to display the drop-down list of file formats. Click either **Compuserve GIF** or **JPEG**. Then click **Save**.

13 In the File Format dialog box, click **OK** to save the image to the folder you selected.

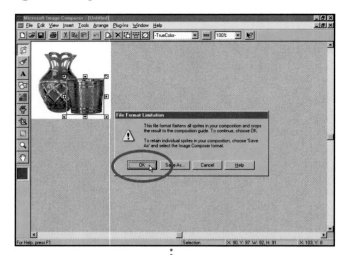

Puzzled?

On the File menu there's a Send to FrontPage option. This option isn't available with a brand new image. You have to save the image to a file before you can get it onto the page.

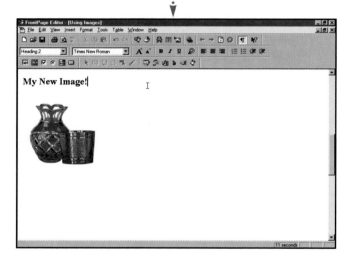

14 Use the methods you learned in Task 39 to import the new image into your Web. Then insert the image onto the page. ■

Missing Link

If you save the new image as a GIF, and you've used more than one image to compose it, you'll get a "File Format Limitation" warning dialog box when you go to save the image. This warning simply means the new, composite GIF image won't retain the independence of the images that you used to make it—you can't later move them around or edit them separately. For our example, just click **OK**.

TASK **48**

Changing a Graphic's Appearance with Image Composer

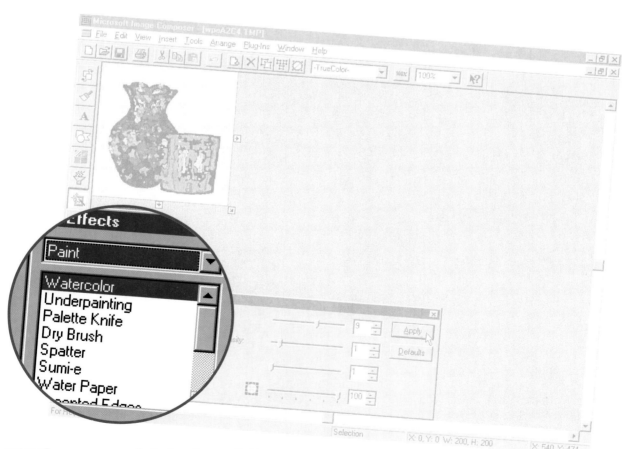

"Why would I do this?"

To add visual variety and texture to your Web graphics, you can use Image Composer's toolbox of effects. With these, you can make an image look like a watercolor, a fresco, an Impressionist painting, or just about anything else you could desire. These effects can make your images much more striking and interesting to your visitors.

1 The illustrations in this example show an image that has been saved in the Web's images/ folder. The image has already been inserted into a Web page, and the page has been saved.

In FrontPage Editor, open the page that has the image you want to modify. Double-click the image.

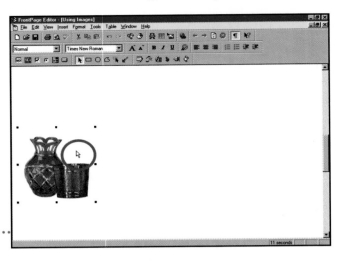

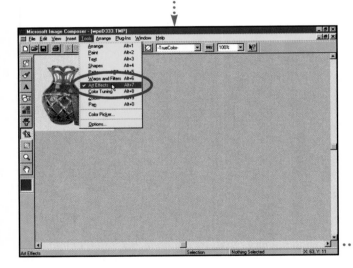

2 When Image Composer opens and displays the image, you can close the Arrange dialog box; you won't need it. Now, we'll change the image to look like a watercolor. Open the **Tools** menu and click **Art Effects**.

3 The Art Effects drop-down list box automatically displays Paint. You can click the arrow button beside the box for a drop-down list of other effects, but for this example we'll stick with Paint. In the larger list box, choose one of the paint effects to apply to the image. The example uses **Watercolor**. After clicking the effect you want, click **Apply**. You'll see the image change. Click the close button in the dialog box's upper-right corner to close it.

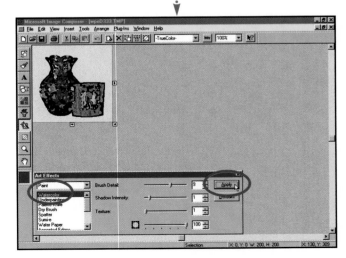

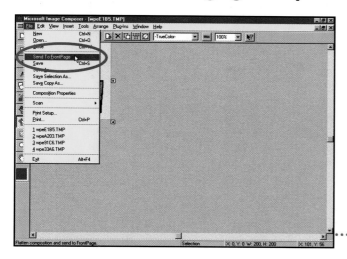

4 Open the **File** menu and click the **Send to FrontPage** option.

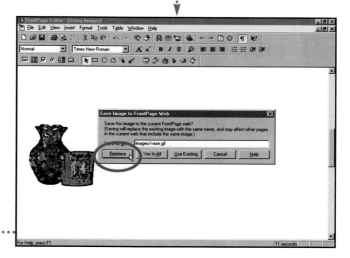

5 The FrontPage Editor workspace appears with the modified image. Click anywhere outside the image to deselect it. Then, open the **File** menu and click the **Save** option. In the Save Image to FrontPage Web dialog box, click **Replace**. This replaces the unmodified file in the Web's images/ folder with the new, modified one.

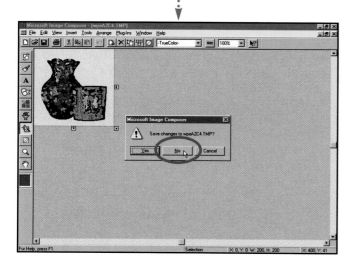

6 Image Composer is still running. Use the Windows 95 Taskbar to switch to it, then open Image Composer's **File** menu and click the **Exit** option. When the Image Composer exit dialog box appears, it will ask if you want to save a file. This is a temporary file it used while working with the original image. Click **No** and Image Composer shuts down. ■

TASK 49

Adding a Sound File to a Page

re's Some Music!

"Why would I do this?"

A bit of well-chosen sound can enhance your page, at least for people who have browsers and PCs that handle audio. The problem is that even a few seconds' worth of audio takes a significant time to load into a browser. Test your audio files to make sure they don't take forever to download.

There are lots of places on the World Wide Web to find audio files you can download. Try:

http://www.yahoo.com/Computers_ and_Internet/Multimedia/Sound/ Archives/

for a start. A standard sound format is WAV; you recognize these by their .wav file name extensions.

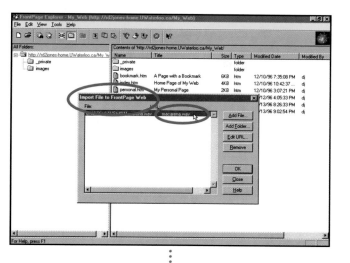

1 Once you've put some sound files into a folder on your PC, import the ones you want into your Web by using FrontPage Explorer's Import option, as you did in Task 39. (The type of file—image, video, sound, or whatever—doesn't matter to Import.)

Missing Link

You can recognize other sound file formats from the file name extensions. Apart from .wav, some common ones are .au, .mid, .snd, and .aif.

2 Then, in FrontPage Editor, open the page where you want the sound. Type some text or insert an image to be the link to the file. Select the text or image. Open the **Edit** menu and click **Hyperlink**.

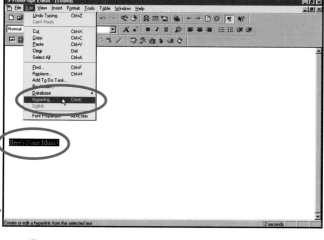

3 In the Create Hyperlink dialog box, use the Current FrontPage Web sheet to locate the sound file you imported. Select the file and click **OK**. Click **OK** again to close the Create Hyperlink dialog box.

Missing Link

Microsoft Internet Explorer 3.0 can use Background Sound. To put Background sound on a page, click **Insert**, then **Background Sound**, and supply the name of the sound file.

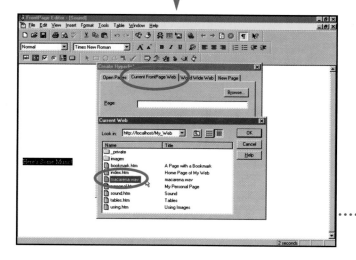

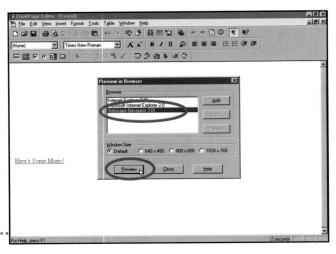

4 To hear and see the results, open the **File** menu and click the **Preview in Browser** option. Select a browser and click **Preview**. When the page appears in the browser window, click the link.

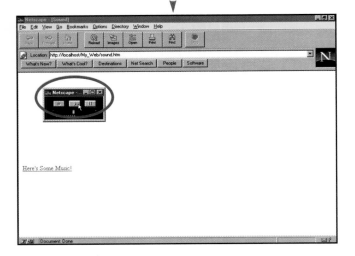

5 An audio player appears in the browser window, and the sound file plays automatically. When you've heard enough, you can close the audio player and then close the browser. (The appearance of the audio player varies from browser to browser.) ■

Missing Link

Remember this kind of testing gives very fast responses. (For more accuracy about loading times for files, use the methods in Task 12, "Viewing Your Web over the Internet.") Keep sound file sizes to less than 20K so they'll download reasonably quickly. Also avoid playing background sounds over and over again, as this gets irritating for many people. Finally, for the same file size, you'll get more sound with a .mid file than with a .wav file.

Adding a Video Clip to a Page

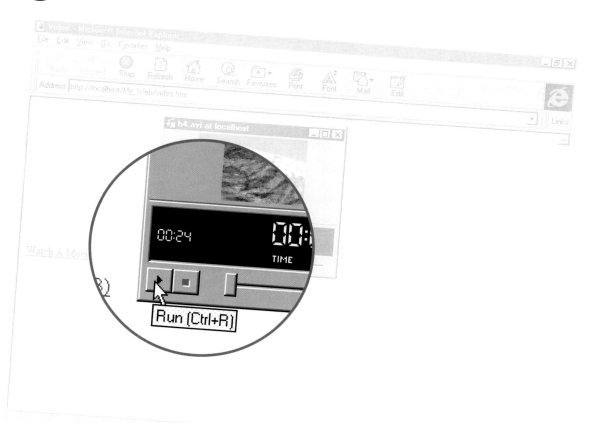

"Why would I do this?"

Video clips add interest to the page; lots of people like to watch a mini-movie. The files all have one thing in common: They're big, and they have to be downloaded to a PC before people can view them. When linking to such a file, you should indicate how big it is, so people can

decide whether they want to download it. You can find video files for testing at:

**http://www.yahoo.com/Computers_
and_Internet/Multimedia/Video**

Some common extensions for video files are .mpg, .mpeg, and .avi.

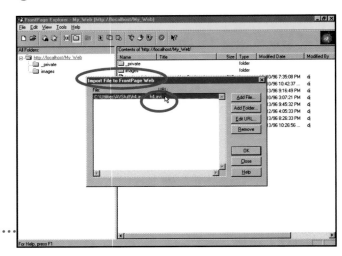

1 Once you've put some video files into a folder on your PC, import the ones you want into your Web by using FrontPage Explorer's Import option, as you did in Task 39.

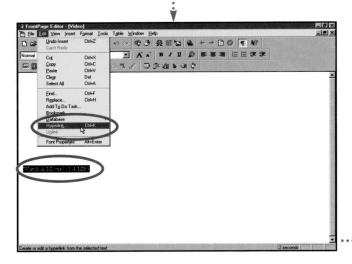

2 Then, in FrontPage Editor, open the page where you want the video to be viewed. Type some text or insert an image to be the link to the file. Remember to tell your viewers how big the file is, so they can decide if they want to download it. Then select the text or image. Open the **Edit** menu and click **Hyperlink**.

3 In the Create Hyperlink dialog box, use the Current FrontPage Web sheet to locate the video file you imported. Select the file, and click **OK**. Click **OK** again to close the Create Hyperlink dialog box.

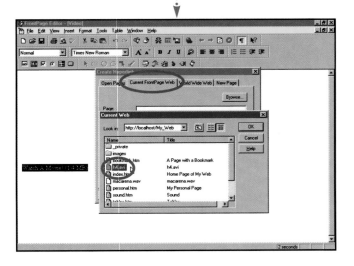

Missing Link

Microsoft Internet Explorer 3.0 can use inline video with AVI files (only). To put inline video on a page, click **Insert**, then **Video**, and supply the name of the AVI file. Internet Explorer 3.0 users will see the video as soon as the page opens, without clicking a link. Other browsers display only a placeholder.

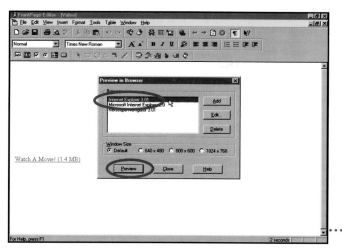

4 To see the results, open the **File** menu and click the **Preview in Browser** option. Select a browser and click **Preview**. When the page appears in the browser window, click the link.

5 In Internet Explorer 3.0 a video player appears in the browser window, and you control the player with its buttons. Netscape Navigator displays AVIs as the picture alone; click it to start and stop playback. When you've seen enough, you can close the video player and then close the browser. ■

Puzzled?

If you tried to preview an .mpg file in Netscape, you may have received an "Unknown File Type" message from the browser. This means you need to download a Netscape plug-in to let you play back this kind of file. Point your browser to **www.netscape.com** and search its site for MPEG plug-ins.

PART V

Working with Tables

IN PART V OF THIS BOOK, YOU LEARN about tables—creating them, changing their appearance and layout, giving them color, and integrating other Web page elements into them.

Tables are a powerful method of arranging and presenting page content. They're especially useful in the World Wide Web environment because of the limitations of our hardware. Most of us peer at relatively small screens, and a screen's resolution is much less than that of a printed page. So any tool that helps us squash information into small, organized areas is a very useful one.

Tables are supported by all the major graphical browsers (Netscape 2.0 and 3.0, Internet Explorer 2.0 and 3.0, and Mosaic 2.1), so feel free to include them in your pages. Different browsers treat visible cell borders differently, though, so you should check to see what the borders look like in each browser before you settle on a design. Equally important, remember that many people cruise the Web at 640×480 resolution; if you create tables that take advantage of the width of a 1024×768 display, your visitors using a lower resolution may not see what you envisioned.

What are tables good for? Well, for just about anything that can be usefully ordered into rows and columns. In a Web page, a cell of a table can contain anything a Web page can contain—images, links, image maps, and so on. Here are some ideas:

- Arrange text in newspaper-like columns. This gives a "newsy" flavor to the page, which suggests to your viewer that your site is always up to date.

- Organize image-based links into rows or columns. This is handy for setting up a "navigation button" section at the top or bottom of a page.

- Present tabular data, like budget sheets, personnel lists, or schedules.

- Lay out captions beside images. This technique helps you structure visual and textual information on a page so that your visitors have an easier time grasping the information that you provide.

- Put tables inside table cells. With this technique, you can vary the structure of a table in almost any way you desire.

- Set up two or more bulleted or numbered lists across a page. Again, this helps you organize your information by allowing you to put bulleted or numbered lists side by side. Using tables is the only easy way to achieve this effect, unless you are designing solely for Netscape Navigator 3.0 and use its column extensions.

- Arrange a table of contents. Put the chapter or section numbers into one column of the table and the chapter or section titles into another. Doing this helps keep things neat and tidy.

- Place colored rectangles on a page by adding color to cells without visible borders. This is more than a decorative effect; using different colors can help differentiate between sections of a table, so your visitors can grasp its information more quickly and effectively.

Creating a Table

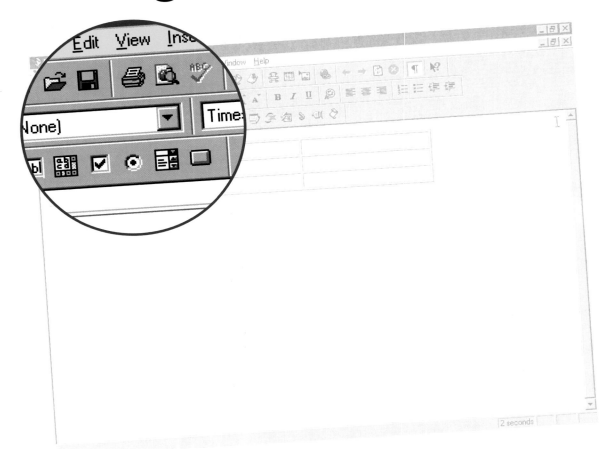

"Why would I do this?"

Tables are commonly placed in Web pages to organize text, images, and links. You can use them to arrange text in parallel columns or to set an explanatory block of text beside the image that resides in the adjacent cell. You can insert lists into cells and you can even insert tables into other tables. All this gives you tremendous flexibility in arranging data and images.

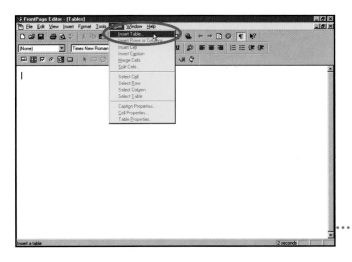

1 Open a page in FrontPage Editor. Click the page where you want the table to appear. (The top-left corner of the table will go where the insertion point is.) Open the **Table** menu and click the **Insert Table** option.

2 In the Size section, type a number into the Rows text box to specify the number of rows in the table. Do the same in the Columns text box.

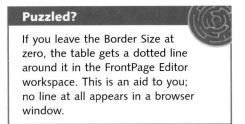

Puzzled?

If you leave the Border Size at zero, the table gets a dotted line around it in the FrontPage Editor workspace. This is an aid to you; no line at all appears in a browser window.

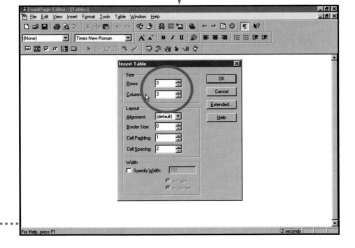

3 In the Layout section, use the Alignment drop-down list box to position the table against the left margin, page center, or right margin. If you want a visible border for the table, type a number into the Border Size text box. In the Cell Padding text box, type a number for the distance between the cell contents and the inside edge of the cell boundary. In the Cell Spacing text box, type a number for the amount of space between cells.

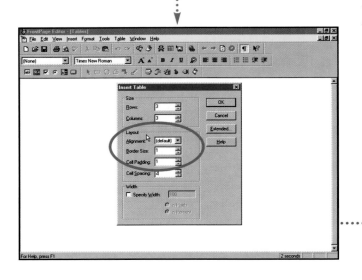

163

4 In the Width section, you can mark the Specify Width check box and then specify how wide you want the table to be. Using "in Percent" is a better choice, because different people use different screen resolutions when browsing. The example table (in the next illustration) has a width of 75 percent.

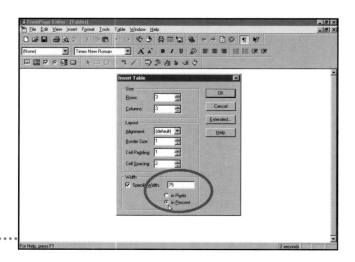

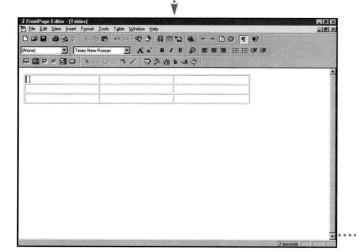

5 Click **OK**. The table appears on the page.

6 To add text to a cell, just click in the cell. Then start typing. If the text line is longer than the width of the cell, the cell will enlarge to move the extra text to the next line within the cell. To delete text in a cell, select the text and press the Delete key. ■

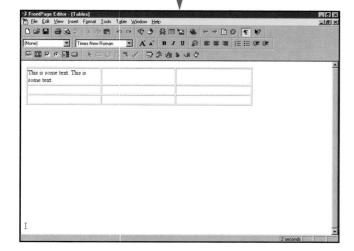

Adding Row and Column Headers

Adams, Bill

Jones, Sam

Smith, Eve

Test 2   Test 3

"Why would I do this?"

As a convenience to users, most tables have column headers to denote the kind of data in each column; many tables also have row headers. An example would be a record of students' grades, with student names as row headers, and assignment titles as column headers.

Task 52: Adding Row and Column Headers

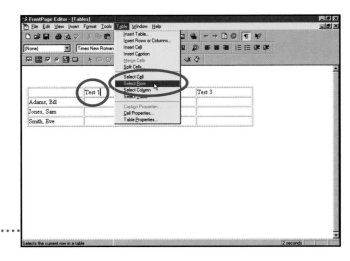

1 To make column headers, click any cell in the top row of the table. Then open the **Table** menu and click the **Select Row** option.

2 With the row selected (it will be black with white text), open the **Table** menu again and click the **Cell Properties** option.

3 In the Cell Properties dialog box, find the Layout section. Click the Header Cell check box to mark it.

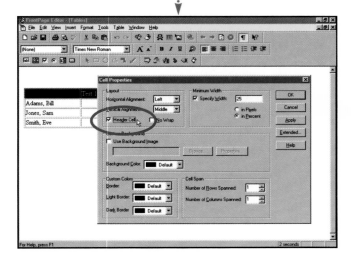

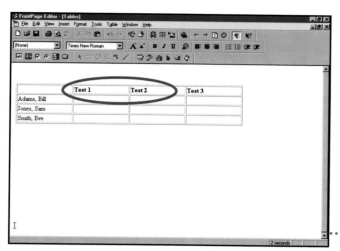

4 Click **OK**. When the Cell Properties dialog box closes, click anywhere outside the table to deselect the row. The text in the column header cells is in Bold.

5 Making row headers resembles the above technique. First, click any cell in the left column. Then open the **Table** menu and click the **Select Row** option. Then repeat Steps 2, 3, and 4. The text in the row header cells will be in bold. ∎

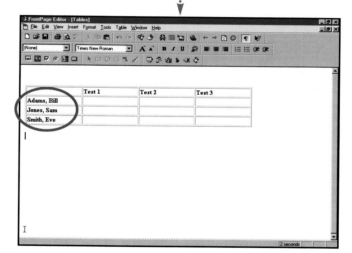

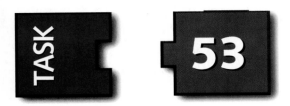

Deleting a Table

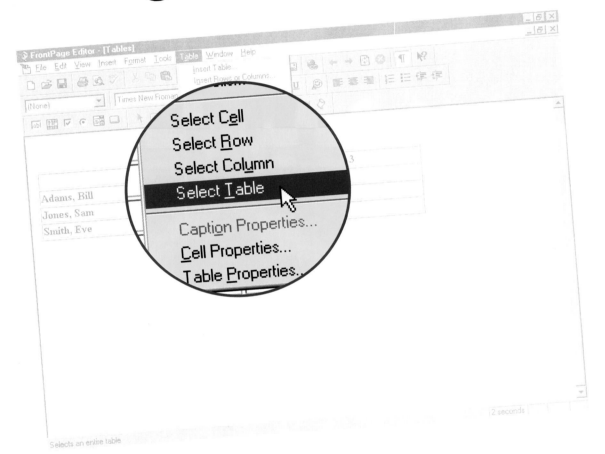

"Why would I do this?"

If you've messed up a table completely, you may want to get rid of it and start over. Or it may simply be obsolete. Fortunately, deleting a table is very straightforward.

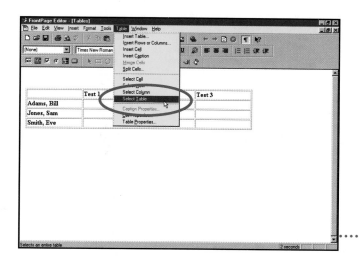

1 Click once in any cell of the table. Then open the **Table** menu and click the **Select Table** option.

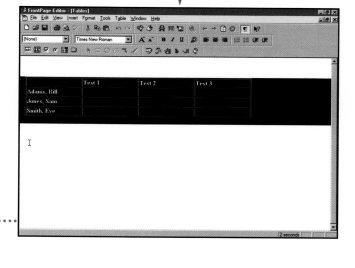

2 The table appears in reverse video (black on white). Press the **Delete** key to delete it.

3 To delete a cell, a row, or a column, first click in the cell, row, or column you want to delete. Open the **Table** menu, then click **Select Cell**, **Select Row**, or **Select Column**. With the cell, row, or column selected, press the **Delete** key. (In the example, the right-most column is to be deleted.) ■

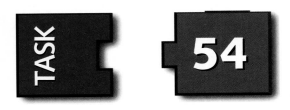

Aligning Cell Content

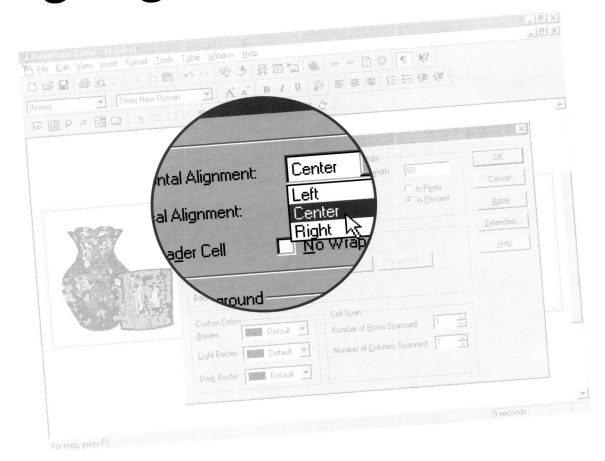

"Why would I do this?"

Depending on your cell content, you may want it positioned in different places. An image, for example, usually looks better if it's centered within the cell borders. Numbers look better against the right edge of a cell, while text is often either at the left or centered. You can also set vertical alignment with the cell content at the middle, top, or bottom of the cell.

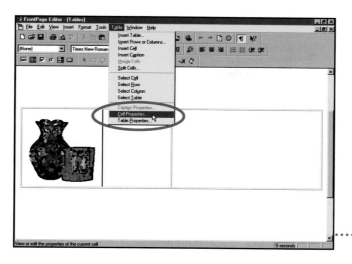

1 Click once in the cell whose content you want to align. Then open the **Table** menu and click the **Cell Properties** option.

2 In the Cell Properties dialog box, look in the Layout section. To align cell content horizontally, click the button at the right of the Horizontal Alignment drop-down list box, and select either **Left**, **Center**, or **Right** from the drop-down list. Use the same method to set vertical alignment with the Vertical Alignment drop-down list. When you've set your alignments, click **OK**.

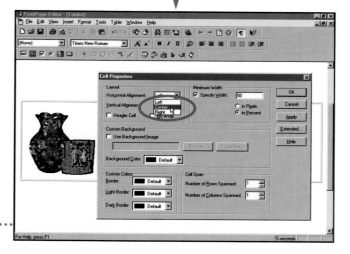

3 The image repositions according to the values you set. ■

Missing Link

You can align the content of all cells in a row, column, or table at once. To align a row, open the **Table** menu and click **Select Row**. Then repeat Step 2. Use the Select Column or Select Table options on the Table menu similarly.

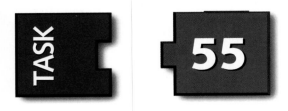

Adding Rows or Columns

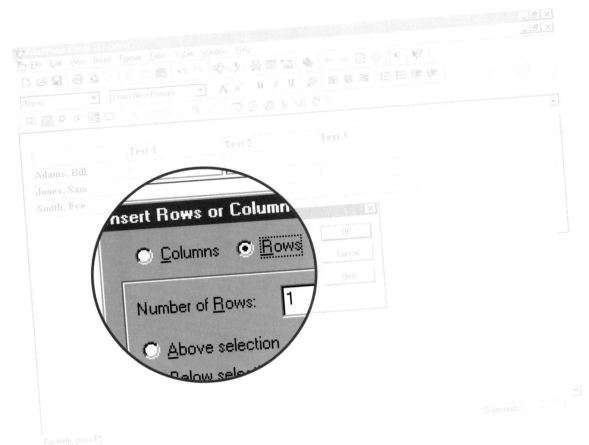

"Why would I do this?"

Even if you've planned your table carefully, you may discover you didn't allow for a certain class of information, and you need to add a row or column for it. Or you may want a set of subheadings running across the width of your table. The following task shows you how to do this.

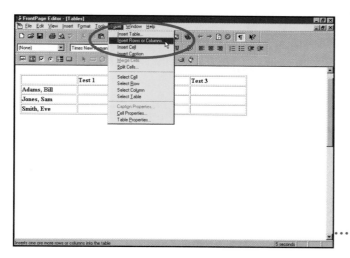

1 To add a row, click in any row that will be adjacent to the new row. Then, open the **Table** menu, and click the **Insert Rows or Columns** option. In the example, we're going to add a row above "Jones, Sam."

2 In the Insert Rows or Columns dialog box, mark the Rows radio button if it isn't already marked. In the Number of Rows text box, type the number of rows you're going to add. Then mark either the Above Selection radio button or the Below Selection radio button. Since the "Jones, Sam" cell was the one we clicked in (it's the selection), and we want to add a row above Sam's, we'll mark the Above Selection radio button.

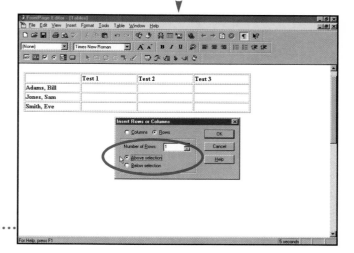

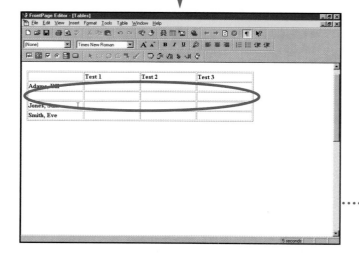

3 Click **OK**. The dialog box closes, and the table has a new row.

4 Adding a new column is a little trickier. Suppose we want to add a column to the right edge of a table. Click anywhere in the right-most column of the table. Then repeat Step 1 to open the Insert Rows or Columns dialog box. Mark the Columns radio button, then mark the Right of Selection radio button if it isn't already marked.

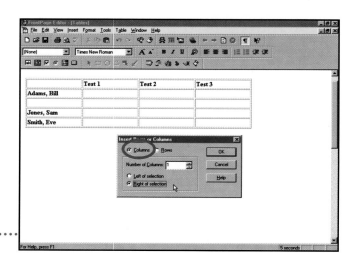

5 Click **OK**. The dialog box closes, and the table has a new column. Unfortunately, it's too narrow, so we'll have to adjust it. Figure out roughly the percentage of the table width it should be; for a five-column table, for example, the column width might be 20 percent (depending on its intended content).

6 Click anywhere in the new column. Then open the **Table** menu and click the **Select Column** option. With the column selected, open the **Table** menu again and click the **Cell Properties** option.

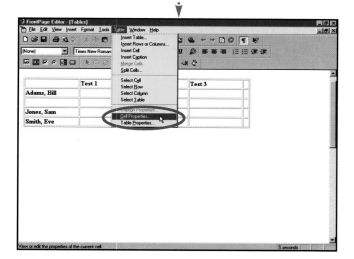

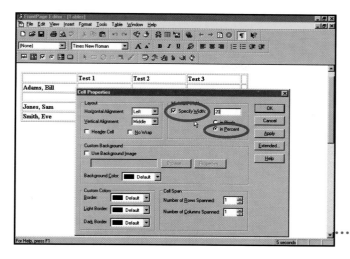

7 Find the Minimum Width section in the Cell Properties dialog box. Mark the Specify Width check box, then the In Percent radio button. Then type the percentage number you worked out in Step 5 into the Specify Width text box. Then click **OK**.

8 The resized table appears. To get it exactly right, you may want to repeat Steps 6 and 7 for each column of the table, adjusting each width until the table looks the way it should. ■

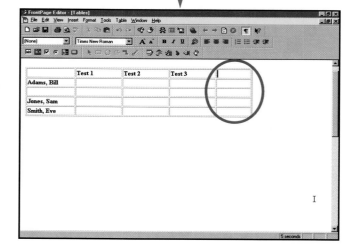

56

Inserting a Cell

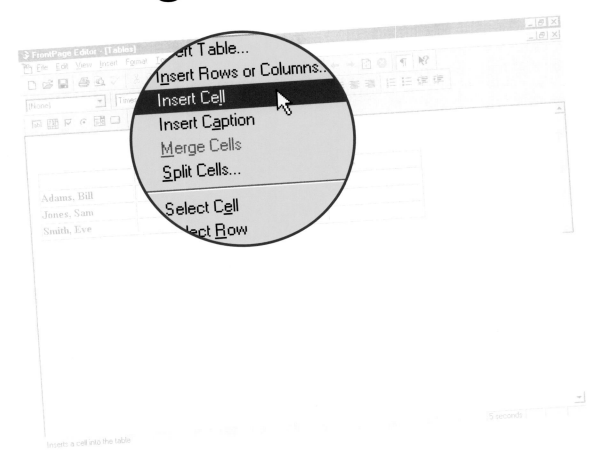

"Why would I do this?"

Sometimes, a table's layout is improved if single cells are inserted into it, rather than inserting whole columns or rows. This isn't likely to happen often, but when you need the effect, here's how to do it.

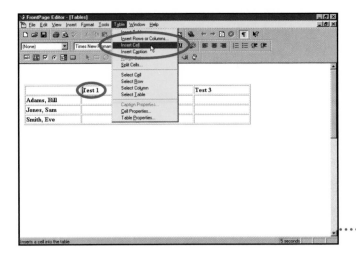

1 Click a cell in a table. To insert a new cell left of this cell, position the insertion point at the left of any data in the cell. To insert the new cell to the right of this cell, place the insertion point at the right of the data. (If the cell is empty, the new cell is inserted at the left.) Open the **Table** menu and click the **Insert Cell** option.

2 The dialog box closes, and the new cell appears in the table. ■

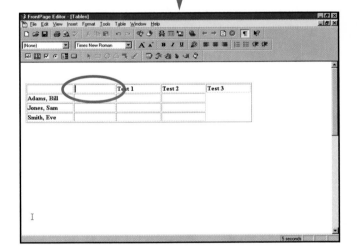

Puzzled?

If you decide you don't want the cell after all, click in it, open the **Table** menu, click **Select Cell**, and press the **Delete** key.

Splitting a Cell

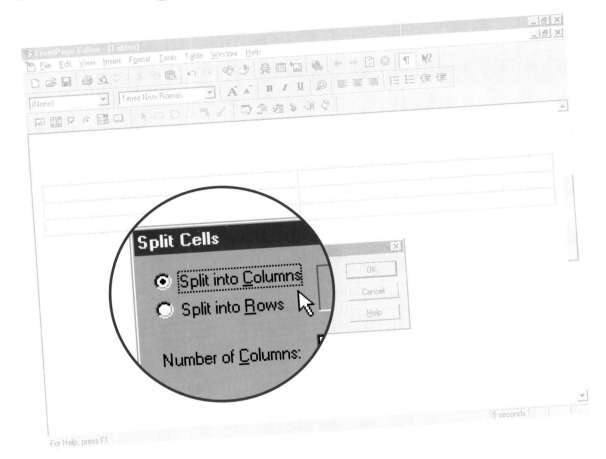

"Why would I do this?"

A regular grid of cells with each column one-cell wide, may not exactly match the way your data needs to be organized and presented. To change the cell layout to serve your purposes better, you can split cells up.

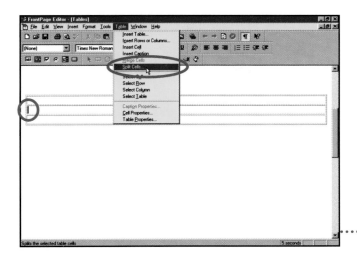

1 Begin by clicking in the cell to be split. Open the **Table** menu, and click **Split Cells**.

2 In the Split Cells dialog box, mark the Split into Columns radio button or Split into Rows radio button, depending on your needs. Then type the number of rows or columns you want into the Number of Columns (or Number of Rows) text box.

Missing Link

If there is data already in the cell, that data is moved to the left-most cell (in column splitting) or upper cell (in row splitting) when the split is completed.

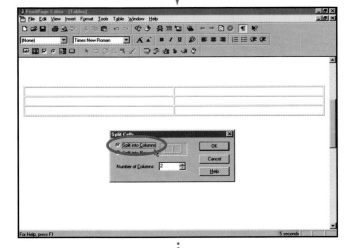

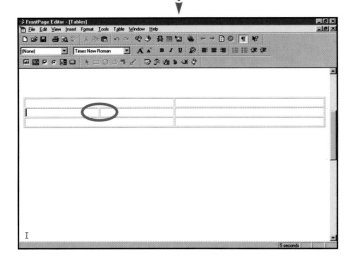

3 Click **OK**. The dialog box closes, and the cell has been split. ■

Puzzled?

If you wish you hadn't split the cell, go on to Task 58, "Merging Cells."

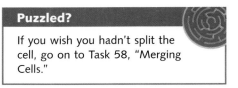

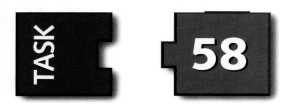

Merging Cells

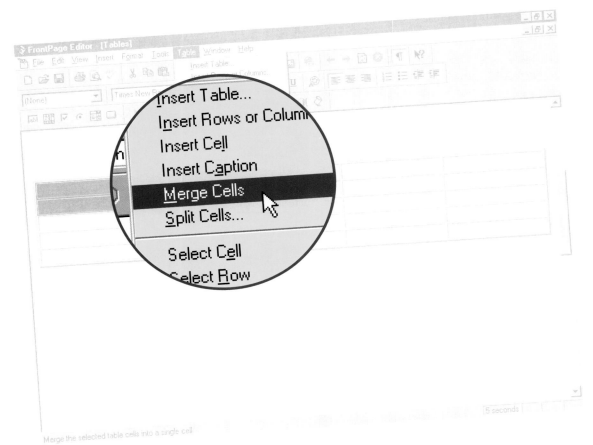

"Why would I do this?"

From time to time a table will look better, and will reflect the organization of your data better, if the cells across two or more columns and/or rows are merged. It's best to plan for this and do it before you have data in the cells—merging occupied cells usually requires you to rearrange the newly combined data or images, too.

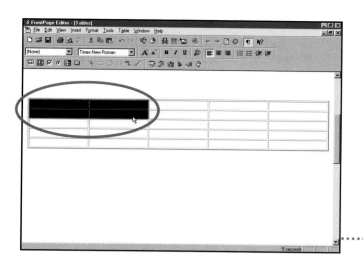

1 Click in one of the cells you want to merge. Then open the **File** menu and click the **Select Cell** option. Hold the Control key down, and click the other cells you want to merge. You can only merge adjacent cells that together form a rectangle.

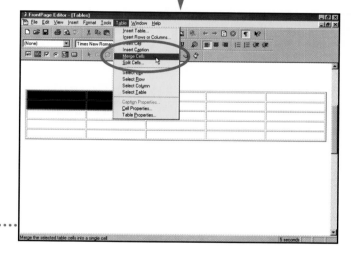

2 Open the **File** menu and click the **Merge Cells** option.

3 The selected cells merge into one. ■

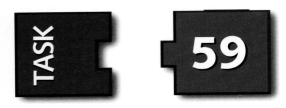

Adding Colors to Your Tables

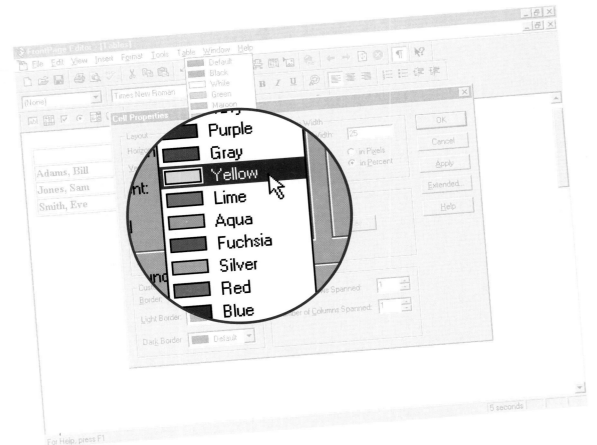

"Why would I do this?"

A plain, black-and-white table may have all the information someone needs, but color will enhance its appeal. This isn't only an aesthetic consideration, either. Emphasizing parts of a table with color can make it easier to understand, and help the viewer get a sense of how the data is organized. A colored header row, for example, will make it clear that this row isn't part of the data.

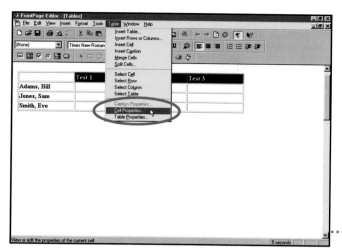

1 Begin by selecting the rows, columns, or cells you want to color. Then open the **File** menu and click the **Cell Properties** option.

2 In the Cell Properties dialog box, click the button at the right of the Background Color drop-down list box. On the drop-down list, click the color you want to apply.

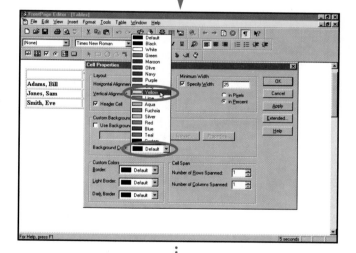

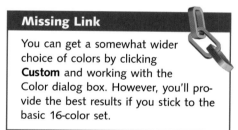

Missing Link

You can get a somewhat wider choice of colors by clicking **Custom** and working with the Color dialog box. However, you'll provide the best results if you stick to the basic 16-color set.

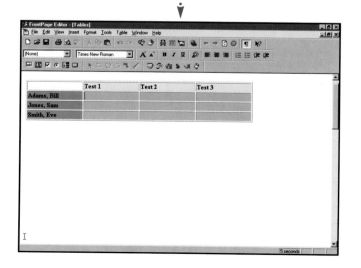

3 Click **OK**. The dialog box closes, and the cell(s), row(s), or column(s) take on their new appearance. ∎

Missing Link

To add a single color to the whole table, click inside the table, then open the **Table** menu and click **Table Properties**. In the Table Properties dialog box, click the button at the right of the Background Color drop-down list box. On the drop-down list, click the color you want to apply. Then click **OK**.

Inserting Page Elements into a Table

"Why would I do this?"

The content of a table isn't restricted to plain text. Cells can include anything that you can put on a Web page—images, image maps, links, and even other tables. Using tables is a fast and accurate way to organize elements on a page; the following are examples of some of the things you can do.

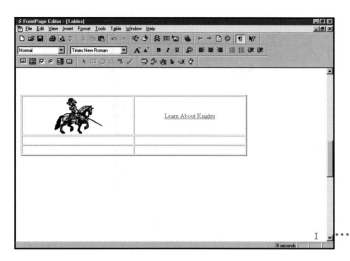

1 Use the methods you learned in Task 39 to add an image to a table. Use the Task-30 method to add a text link as well.

2 Add another image, and use Task 45 to link it to a video clip. Use Task 43 to give the image some alternative text for people who don't see the image, and make a text link to the clip in the right-hand cell of the row.

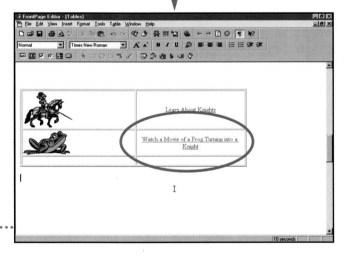

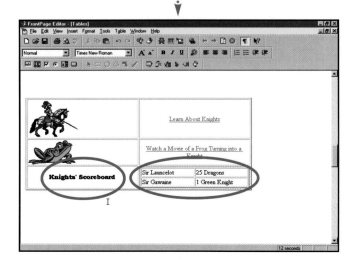

3 Use Task 51 to create another table inside the right-most cell of the third row. Add some text to this minitable. Put a text label in the left-hand cell. Format the label's characters by using the font methods from Task 18. ■

PART VI

Maintaining Your Web

61 Using the To Do List

62 Verifying Hyperlinks

63 Spell Checking Your Web

64 Finding Text in Your Web

65 Replacing Text in Your Web

IN THIS PART YOU LEARN the fundamentals of FrontPage Web site management: using the To Do list, finding, replacing and spell checking across Webs, and verifying and fixing broken links.

Creating and linking pages is only the beginning of a Web site's existence. All sites need to be maintained—pages must be modified, deleted, or added; links have to be updated; the content has to be checked for relevance and timeliness. All this can add up to a significant investment of time, even for a relatively small Web site.

FrontPage 97 has a number of tools that help you maintain your site. The tight integration of FrontPage Editor and FrontPage Explorer makes adding or updating pages a simple

operation (at least in principle) and with the Preview in Browser command at your disposal, there's little excuse for not checking the appearance of your pages. With the To Do List, you can keep track of necessary tasks, and mark them off as you complete them.

Remember to use FrontPage Explorer's Hyperlink view to get a graphical overview of your Web. This will help you keep your Web pages properly related to each other. With respect to links, make regular use of the Verify Hyperlinks command to check for and repair broken links. The Find command, the Replace command, and the Spell checker will help you keep the text elements of your Web consistent and professional.

Maintaining content is less cut and dried. A lot of people set up Web sites and then pay little attention to them; in Web jargon, these are "stale sites." The frequency with which you need to update your Web's content will, of course, depend on what you designed your Web to do. If it's a repository of long-lived documents, the information in the documents themselves will obviously not change. However, your site will be more lively if you keep looking for new information and adding it to existing pages or creating new ones for it. Then, after you've collected a certain amount of material, you may realize that the information would be more useful if it were organized differently. To announce such changes, you'd use a "What's New" page.

At the other end of the spectrum, you may have a site whose appeal depends heavily on being up to date with the latest in-fashion technology, music, business, or whatever. With a site like this, you need to be constantly aware of the major changes in the field with which your site is associated, and keep your information at the cutting edge. And, in this kind of site, it's not just the information that must be updated fast and regularly—your links to related Web sites must also be maintained. This, too, can be considerable work, since, in a fast-changing field, links frequently get changed, moved, or simply vanish. Speaking of vanishing, if you have to move your site from one Web address to another, arrange to have a forwarding address left on the old site for awhile, so people looking for you can update their browser bookmarks.

If you're operating a site that showcases your products or services, you have to make sure your price lists, addresses, ordering information, and product or service descriptions are current. Leaving a forwarding address is even more important for a site like this, if you have to move it.

For better or worse, people are looking for variety and change on the Web. Keep your site interesting, don't let it get stale, and they'll keep coming back to see what you've been up to.

TASK 61

Using the To Do List

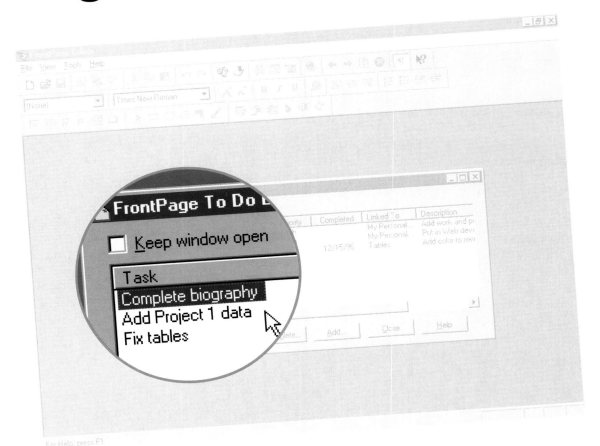

"Why would I do this?"

The To Do List is significantly more powerful than its name suggests. It's actually a decent project management tool, and tells you not only what still has to be done on your site, but also what has been done so far, who did it, and when. If you're building a complex Web, the To Do list will help you avoid overlooking essential tasks.

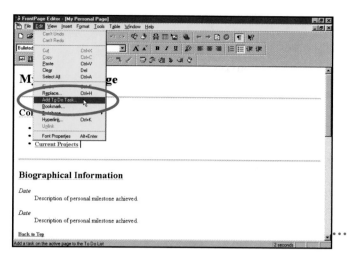

1 Let's assume you have a complicated Web and you want to build a To Do list keyed to its various pages. Open one of these pages in FrontPage Editor. Then open the **Edit** menu and click the **Add To Do Task** option. (The example shows a page created with the Personal Home Page Wizard.)

2 The Add To Do Task dialog box opens. Type a brief name for the task into the Task Name text box. If you like, you can specify the person responsible in the Assign To box. Then type a brief description of the task, if it's needed, into the Description text box. Set a Priority with the radio buttons, then click **OK**. The dialog box closes. Repeat Steps 1 and 2 for this page, and any other pages that need a task list, until you've completed the task list for the Web.

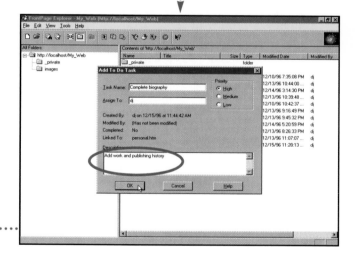

3 Let's suppose you've already composed a task list, as in Steps 1 and 2, and you're starting a FrontPage session to complete some of these tasks. To use the task list as a guide for your work, start FrontPage and open the appropriate Web. In FrontPage Explorer, open the **Tools** menu and click the **Show To Do List** option. (The menu option conveniently shows the number of outstanding tasks.)

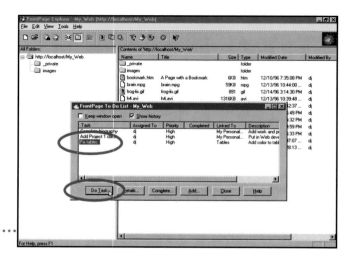

4 The FrontPage To Do List dialog box opens, showing the tasks associated with the whole Web, not with one particular page. (The page the task is for is listed in the Linked To column.) To keep an eye on both complete and incomplete tasks, ensure the Show History check box is marked. Click the name of the task you want to do, and click **Do Task**.

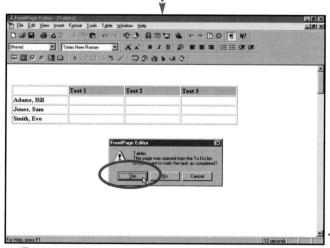

5 The page with the task automatically opens in FrontPage Editor. Complete it, and close or save the page. Whichever you do, you get a dialog box asking if you want to mark the task completed. Click **Yes** or **No**, whichever is appropriate. The To Do list is automatically updated if you clicked Yes.

6 To go on with your list of tasks, you open the FrontPage To Do list from either FrontPage Explorer or FrontPage Editor, by opening the **Tools** menu and clicking the **Show To Do List** option. In the illustration, the "Fix Tables" task is shown as completed.

Puzzled?

You can also open the To Do List from the Tools menu, and use the Add button to add tasks to the list. However, tasks added with the Add button aren't associated with a specific page, so you won't be able to use the Do Task button later to get at that particular task.

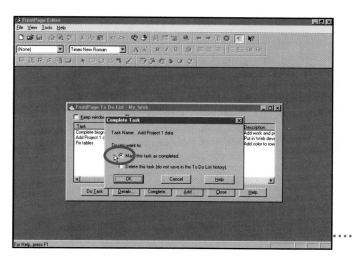

7 To manually mark a task completed by using the FrontPage To Do List dialog box, click the task name, then click **Completed**. In the Complete Task dialog box you can elect to save or not save its record in the To Do List history, by marking the appropriate radio buttons. When you've done so, click **OK**.

8 To modify the task description, click the name of the task, then click **Details**. In the Task Details dialog box, type the new information into the Task Name, Assign To, and Description text boxes. Change the Priority with the radio buttons, and click **OK**.

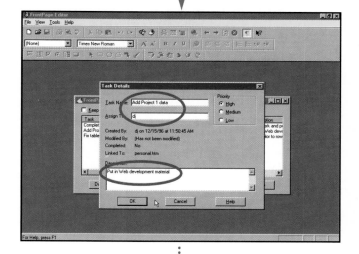

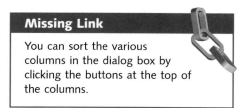

Missing Link

You can sort the various columns in the dialog box by clicking the buttons at the top of the columns.

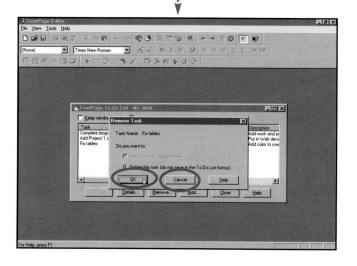

9 To remove a completed task from the list, click its name and click **Remove**. There isn't really a choice in the Remove Task dialog box; click **OK** to remove the task's record, or **Cancel** to cancel the Remove action. ■

62

Verifying Hyperlinks

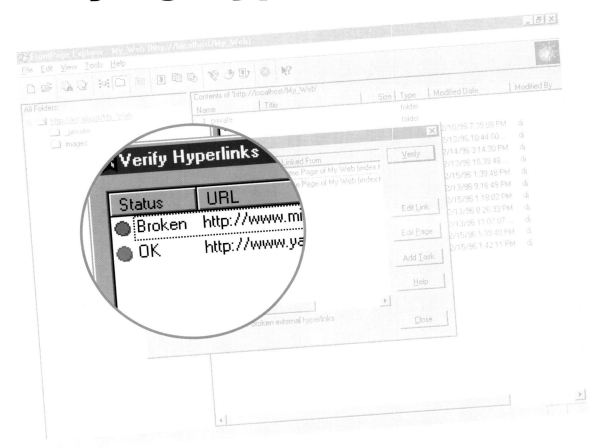

"Why would I do this?"

Maintaining your Web's links, both those within the FrontPage Web itself, and those to sites out on the World Wide Web, is important. Links get broken for three main reasons: a page file name (URL) changes, a page is deleted, or you mistakenly edit the link so that it refers to a nonexistent or incorrect Web address. Even if you don't change your own Web, you should routinely check to make sure its links to sites on the World Wide Web are intact. And, whenever you do modify your Web, run a check of the links. This way your visitors will never encounter the infuriating "404 Not Found" error, at least not on your Web.

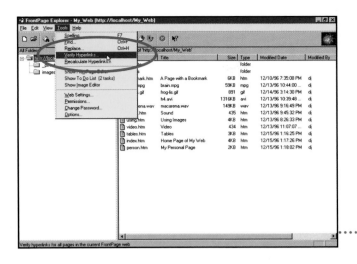

1 To check just the internal links of a Web, start FrontPage and open the Web in question. (If this Web is already open, be sure to save all open pages before running the check.) Then open the **Tools** menu and click **Verify Hyperlinks**.

2 The Verify Hyperlink dialog box opens. Broken links within the open Web are marked with a red dot. Since the PC was not connected to the Internet for this check, the external links have yellow dots to show they weren't checked. The URL column lists the hyperlink being verified; the Linked From column lists the pages containing the broken link. To fix a broken link, click the name of the broken link. Then click **Edit Link**.

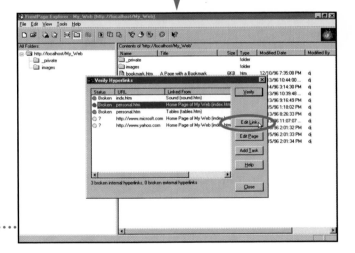

3 In the Edit Link dialog box, type the correct link into the **With** text box. If several pages have the bad link, you can change them all at once by marking the Change All Pages with This Hyperlink radio button. When you've finished, click **OK**.

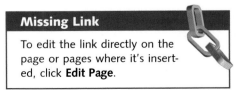

Missing Link

To edit the link directly on the page or pages where it's inserted, click **Edit Page**.

193

4 The Edit Link dialog box closes. Now, in the Verify Hyperlinks dialog box, you see that the earlier broken links are listed as Edited. Repeat Step 3 until all the bad links have been fixed. Click **Close**, then open the **Tools** menu and click **Verify Hyperlinks** again. All the bad links will be gone, though the external links to the World Wide Web will still be marked in yellow.

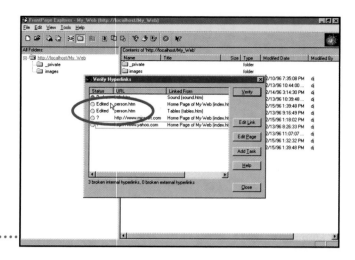

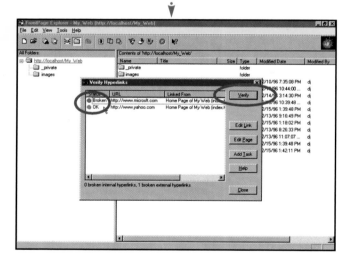

5 To verify the external links, begin by opening your PC's connection to the Internet. Then, in FrontPage Explorer, open the Web to be checked. Open the **Tools** menu and click **Verify Hyperlinks**. The external links aren't checked automatically; to begin the process, click the **Verify** button. When the checking finishes, you see red dots for broken links, green dots for good ones. Carry out Step 3 as needed to repair the links. ■

Puzzled?

Verifying a large number of external links can take a long time. While it's going on, the Verify button changes to a Stop button. Click this button to stop the verification process.

Spell Checking Your Web

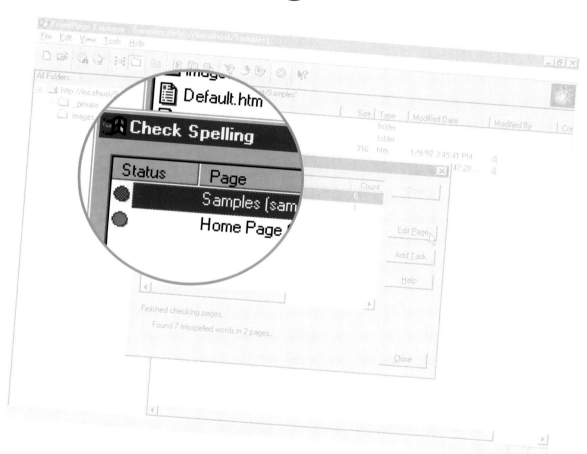

"Why would I do this?"

This option is great if you can't remember how many or which of the 67 pages you've actually spell checked in your new Web. It inspects every page of a Web for errors, and helps you either change them en masse, or make note of them in the To Do list so you can clean up the problems later.

Task 63: Spell Checking Your Web

1 Begin by opening the FrontPage Web you want to spell check. Or, if you've already been editing a Web's pages in FrontPage Editor, save all the open pages before proceeding to do the spell check. Then, if you're not already there, switch to FrontPage Explorer. (If you want to check just some of the pages instead of all of them, use the right pane of FrontPage Explorer's Folder View to select these pages). Then open the **Tools** menu and click **Spelling**.

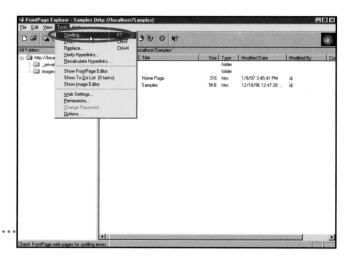

2 In the Spelling dialog box, mark the Add Pages with Misspellings to the To Do List check box ONLY if you want to merely note which pages need attention to their spelling. (Selecting this option simply adds a task to the To Do list, if a page with a misspelling is found. The option to correct the page isn't offered.) If you want to correct the spelling now, leave this checkbox blank and click **Start**.

3 In the Check Spelling dialog box, a list of pages containing errors appears, with each Page Title having a red dot beside it. Click the first Page Title and click **Edit Page**. FrontPage Editor opens the page, and the Spelling dialog box appears. This is the same dialog box you saw in Task 26, "Spell Checking Your Work." Use the techniques you learned in that task to correct errors.

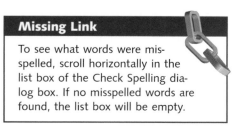

Missing Link

To see what words were misspelled, scroll horizontally in the list box of the Check Spelling dialog box. If no misspelled words are found, the list box will be empty.

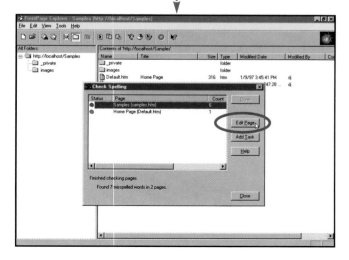

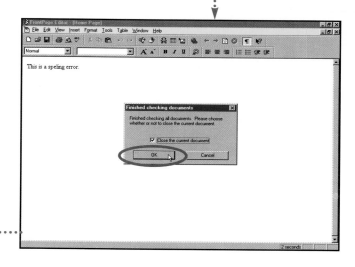

4 If there's more than one page with spelling errors, then the Continue with Next Document dialog box appears when you reach the end of the page. (If there's only one page with errors, go now to Step 5.) Assuming you want to go on making corrections, leave the Close the Current Document check box marked, and click **Next Document**. The next page containing errors appears, with the Spelling dialog box displayed, as in Step 3. Repeat Steps 3 and 4 until you've corrected all the pages.

5 When you've finished correcting the final page containing errors, the Finished Checking Documents dialog box appears. Leave the Close the Current Document check box marked, and click **OK**.

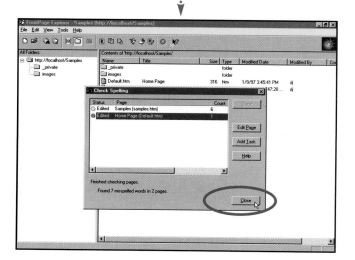

6 Switch to the FrontPage Explorer window. The Check Spelling dialog box now has yellow dots and the word "Edited" beside each page listed in the list box. Click **Close** to leave the spell-checking operation. ■

Finding Text in Your Web

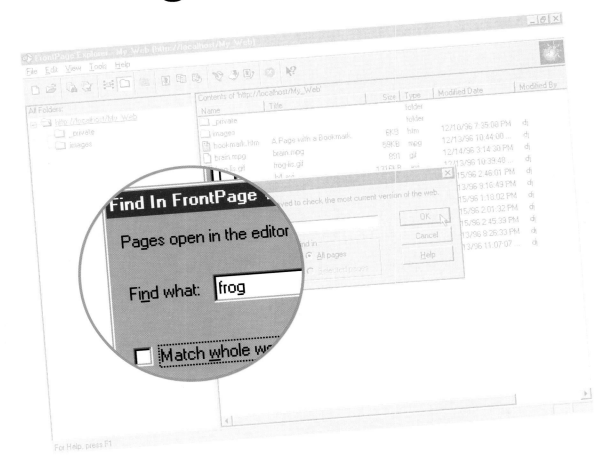

"Why would I do this?"

Like FrontPage Editor, FrontPage Explorer has a Find command. Use it to search for occurrences of a particular word or phrase.

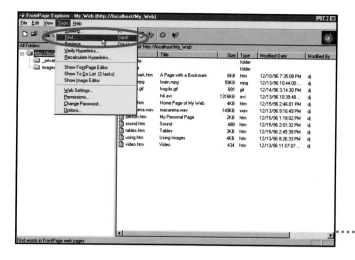

1 Before beginning, save all opened pages in your Web, because Find checks the files on the disk, not the documents opened in FrontPage Editor's workspace. To search only some pages of the Web, select them in the right pane of Folder View; if none are selected, they're all searched. Then, open the **Tools** menu and click **Find**.

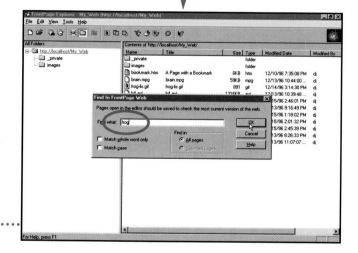

2 In the Find in FrontPage Web dialog box, type the word or phrase you want to find. Mark the Match Whole Word Only check box and/or the Match Case check box if appropriate. If you're searching selected pages, make sure the Selected Pages radio button is marked; to search all pages, mark the All Pages radio button. Then click **OK**.

3 The Find Occurrences dialog box opens, with a list of the pages on which the word was found and the number of times it was found on each page. Click the first name in the list, then click **Edit Page**.

4 The page opens in FrontPage Editor, with the Find dialog box displayed, and the first occurrence of the word highlighted. To go on to the next occurrence of the word, click **Find Next** in the Find dialog box. (If you want to stop and work on the page, click outside the Find dialog box and do so; then click inside the dialog box to activate it again.) Eventually, you reach the end of the page. If you're checking multiple pages, continue with Step 5; if only one page, go to Step 6.

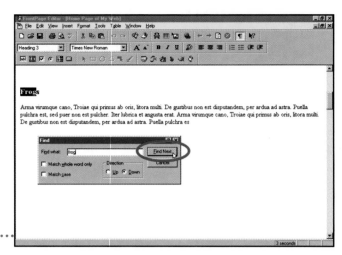

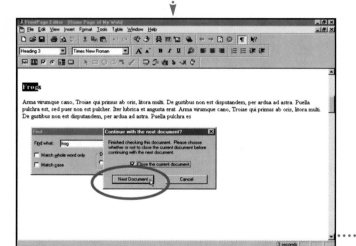

5 When you reach the end of the page, the Continue with Next Document dialog box appears. Leave the Save and Close the Current Document check box marked and click **Next Document**. The next page containing the found word opens. Repeat the search process until you've searched all the pages.

6 After all the pages are searched, the Finished Checking Documents dialog box appears. Leave the Save and Close the Current Document check box marked, and click **OK**. You'll still be in FrontPage Editor. Close FrontPage Editor to return to FrontPage Explorer, and in FrontPage Explorer close the Find Occurrences dialog box. ■

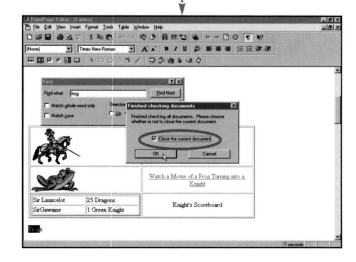

Replacing Text in Your Web

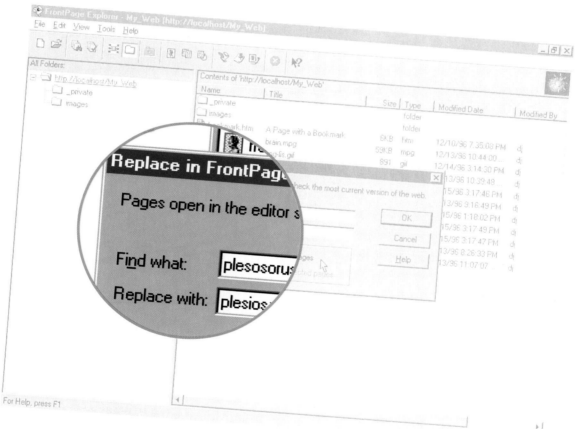

"Why would I do this?"

This is particularly useful when you discover you didn't actually know how to spell "plesiosaurus," and you probably used the word a couple of dozen times throughout your Web (this is just an example, OK?). Using Front-Page Explorer's Replace command will allow you to change every occurrence of "plesosorus" to the correct spelling of the word.

However, *don't* use Replace to replace the text of a link. Doing so destroys the link.

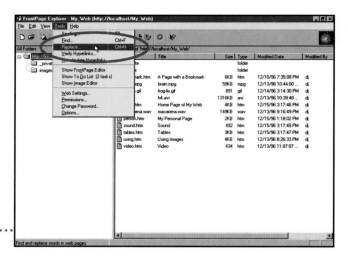

1 Before beginning, save all open pages in your Web, because Replace checks the files on the disk, not the documents opened in FrontPage Editor's workspace. To search only some pages of the Web, select them in the right pane of Folder View; if none are selected, they're all searched. Then open the **Tools** menu and click the **Replace** option to open the Replace in FrontPage Web dialog box.

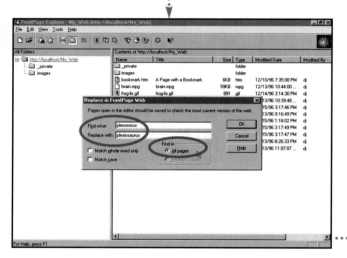

2 Type the word or phrase you want to replace into the Find What text box, and its replacement into the Replace With text box. Mark the Match Whole Word Only check box and/or the Match Case check box if appropriate. If you're working with selected pages, make sure the Selected Pages radio button is marked; to replace across the whole Web, mark the All Pages radio button. Then click **OK**.

3 The Find Occurrence dialog box opens with a list of the pages on which the word was found and the number of times it was found on each page. Click the first name on the list, then click **Edit Page**.

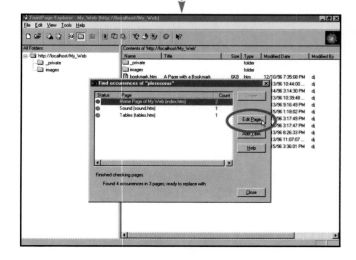

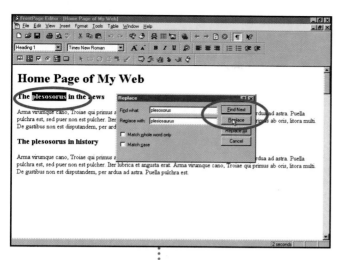

4 The selected page opens, with the Replace dialog box displayed, and the first occurrence of the word highlighted. If you want to change it, click **Replace**. Then click **Find Next** to go on searching. If you decide not to change this occurrence, click **Find Next** instead of **Replace**. If you're brave, click **Replace All** to automatically make the changes across the entire page. Eventually you reach the end of the page. If you're checking multiple pages, continue with Step 5; if only one page, go to Step 6.

5 When you reach the end of the page, the Continue with Next Document dialog box appears. Leave the Save and Close the Current Document check box marked and click **Next Document.** The next page containing the found word opens. Repeat the replacement process until you've done the replace on all the pages.

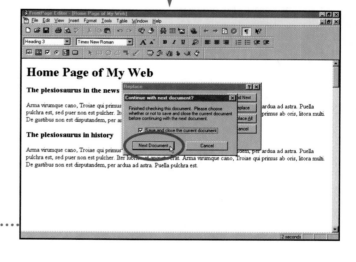

6 After all the pages are checked, the Finished Checking Documents dialog box appears. Leave the Save and Close the Current Document check box marked, and click **OK**. You'll still be in FrontPage Editor. Close FrontPage Editor to return to FrontPage Explorer, and in FrontPage Explorer close the Find Occurrences dialog box. ∎

Index

Symbols

A

B

C

Index

Index

X - Y - Z

Complete and Return this Card
for a *FREE* Computer Book Catalog

Thank you for purchasing this book! You have purchased a superior computer book written expressly for your needs. To continue to provide the kind of up-to-date, pertinent coverage you've come to expect from us, we need to hear from you. Please take a minute to complete and return this self-addressed, postage-paid form. In return, we'll send you a free catalog of all our computer books on topics ranging from word processing to programming and the internet.

Mr. ☐   Mrs. ☐   Ms. ☐   Dr. ☐

Name (first) ☐☐☐☐☐☐☐☐☐☐☐☐ (M.I.) ☐ (last) ☐☐☐☐☐☐☐☐☐☐☐☐☐☐☐☐☐☐

Address ☐☐☐☐☐☐☐☐☐☐☐☐☐☐☐☐☐☐☐☐☐☐☐☐☐☐☐☐☐☐☐☐☐

☐☐☐☐☐☐☐☐☐☐☐☐☐☐☐☐☐☐☐☐☐☐☐☐☐☐☐☐☐☐☐☐☐

City ☐☐☐☐☐☐☐☐☐☐☐☐☐☐☐☐☐☐ State ☐☐ Zip ☐☐☐☐☐ ☐☐☐

Phone ☐☐☐ ☐☐☐ ☐☐☐☐ Fax ☐☐☐ ☐☐☐ ☐☐☐☐

Company Name ☐☐☐☐☐☐☐☐☐☐☐☐☐☐☐☐☐☐☐☐☐☐☐☐☐☐☐☐☐☐☐

E-mail address ☐☐☐☐☐☐☐☐☐☐☐☐☐☐☐☐☐☐☐☐☐☐☐☐☐☐☐☐☐☐☐

1. Please check at least (3) influencing factors for purchasing this book.

Front or back cover information on book .... ☐
Special approach to the content .... ☐
Completeness of content .... ☐
Author's reputation .... ☐
Publisher's reputation .... ☐
Book cover design or layout .... ☐
Index or table of contents of book .... ☐
Price of book .... ☐
Special effects, graphics, illustrations .... ☐
Other (Please specify): _____ ☐

2. How did you first learn about this book?

Saw in Macmillan Computer Publishing catalog .... ☐
Recommended by store personnel .... ☐
Saw the book on bookshelf at store .... ☐
Recommended by a friend .... ☐
Received advertisement in the mail .... ☐
Saw an advertisement in: _____ ☐
Read book review in: _____ ☐
Other (Please specify): _____ ☐

3. How many computer books have you purchased in the last six months?

This book only .... ☐   3 to 5 books .... ☐
2 books .... ☐   More than 5 .... ☐

4. Where did you purchase this book?

Bookstore .... ☐
Computer Store .... ☐
Consumer Electronics Store .... ☐
Department Store .... ☐
Office Club .... ☐
Warehouse Club .... ☐
Mail Order .... ☐
Direct from Publisher .... ☐
Internet site .... ☐
Other (Please specify): _____ ☐

5. How long have you been using a computer?

☐ Less than 6 months   ☐ 6 months to a year
☐ 1 to 3 years   ☐ More than 3 years

6. What is your level of experience with personal computers and with the subject of this book?

	With PCs	With subject of book
New	☐	☐
Casual	☐	☐
Accomplished	☐	☐
Expert	☐	☐

Source Code ISBN: 0-7897-1224-5

7. Which of the following best describes your job title?

Administrative Assistant .... ☐
Coordinator .... ☐
Manager/Supervisor .... ☐
Director .... ☐
Vice President .... ☐
President/CEO/COO .... ☐
Lawyer/Doctor/Medical Professional .... ☐
Teacher/Educator/Trainer .... ☐
Engineer/Technician .... ☐
Consultant .... ☐
Not employed/Student/Retired .... ☐
Other (Please specify): _____ ☐

8. Which of the following best describes the area of the company your job title falls under?

Accounting .... ☐
Engineering .... ☐
Manufacturing .... ☐
Operations .... ☐
Marketing .... ☐
Sales .... ☐
Other (Please specify): _____ ☐

9. What is your age?

Under 20 .... ☐
21-29 .... ☐
30-39 .... ☐
40-49 .... ☐
50-59 .... ☐
60-over .... ☐

10. Are you:

Male .... ☐
Female .... ☐

11. Which computer publications do you read regularly? (Please list)

_____
_____
_____
_____
_____
_____
_____
_____
_____
_____
_____

Comments: _____
_____
_____

Fold here and scotch-tape to mail.